D1112845

God's Shrink

GOD'S SHRINK

10 Sessions and Life's Greatest Lessons from an Unexpected Patient

Michael Adamse, Ph.D.

Health Communications, Inc.
Deerfield Beach, Florida

www.hcibooks.com

Library of Congress Cataloging-in-Publication Data

Adamse, Michael.
   God's shrink : 10 sessions and life's greatest lessons from an unexpected
patient / Michael Adamse.
     p. cm.
  ISBN-13: 978-0-7573-0617-4 (trade pbk.)
  ISBN-10: 0-7573-0617-9 (trade pbk.)
  1. Psychotherapy—Fiction.   2. Delusions—Fiction.   I. Title.
PS3551.D39537G63 2007
813'.54—dc22

                                       2007014817

All rights reserved. Printed in the United States of America. No part of this publication may be reproduced, stored in a retrieval system, or transmitted in any
form or by any means, electronic, mechanical, photocopying, recording, or otherwise, without the written permission of the publisher.

HCI, its logos and marks are trademarks of Health Communications, Inc.

Publisher: Health Communications, Inc.
               3201 S.W. 15th Street
               Deerfield Beach, FL 33442-8190

Cover design by Andrea Perrine Brower
Interior design and formatting by Dawn Von Strolley Grove

For Suzanne

Contents

Acknowledgments

The process of writing a book is really a story within a story. What begins as a concept in the author's mind grows slowly at first, one page at a time. Proposals are considered, drafts are written, sections enhanced or discarded, and slowly the momentum continues to build until a polished book emerges from imagination to print.

It rolls off the presses, finds distribution channels, and ultimately lands in the hands of a reader. The book stirs thoughts and emotions in someone's mind and heart. Through the magic of words, the book takes on a new life with every reading.

Far from a solitary endeavor, the writing and publication of *God's Shrink* was a team effort and that's where I found the book to be the most personally meaningful. It is my greatest pleasure to thank everyone connected with this project.

My first expression of gratitude belongs with my wife, Suzanne Harris Adamse, for her ever-present support and belief in me. She provided me with intelligent feedback and unfailing optimism as the book evolved. Thank you, Suzanne.

One of the unusual gifts in my life is the fact that beyond their professional association with me, many of the staff at Health Communications are also my friends.

Allison Janse, my editor at HCI, deserves special recognition for her skills, enthusiasm, and support for the project. Her patience with my obsessive-compulsive traits and her sense of humor were always appreciated. Many thanks go to the rest of the editorial team for their hard work: Michele Matrisciani, Carol Rosenberg, and Katheline St. Fort.

Kim Weiss, my dear friend and publicist at HCI, believed in the book from day one as well. Her excitement and advocacy for the book are of great importance. Thank you, Kim. Kelly Maragni did a great job of tirelessly marketing the book and was also a strong supporter of the project from its beginning.

I also wish to express my gratitude to Lori Golden, Sean Geary, Veronica Blake, Patricia McConnell, Terry York, Jaron Hunter, Paola Fernandez, and all the other staff who helped get the word out. Thank you to Larissa Hise Henoch and all of the production staff for their efforts with cover design, typesetting, and printing.

This is the third occasion that I can thank Peter Vegso, president and publisher of HCI Books, for his support and most important, for the opportunity to share a perspective of God that is somewhat "outside the box." Thanks also to the other members of the executive staff: Tom Sand, Terry Burke, Pat Holdsworth, and Craig Jarvie.

Anthony Flacco provided a fresh perspective and his expert editorial guidance helped to bring the book to a higher level of excellence. His suggestions were invaluable. Thank you, Anthony.

I would also like to express my appreciation to Maria and Engel Adamse, MaryAnne and Thomas Harris, and Elise and Dana Adamse for their support. A special thanks to my lifelong friend J. C. Smith for always encouraging me through the years.

Finally, my most important acknowledgment lies with God, for choreographing all of this.

Prologue

Under normal circumstances, the province of psychotherapy is practiced privately. What is said behind closed doors remains there. The patient can sing like a bird, but the therapist is ethically and legally bound by confidentiality. A brief postscript in a chart may summarize the generalities of what transpired; however, that's about it.

I can truthfully say that in all my years of practice, I only compromised that bond of confidentiality with three patients. The first involved serious child abuse, and the second concerned an individual who was imminently suicidal. These were clearly based on a duty to warn and protect.

The third case, which is the focus of this book, has nothing to do with legalities or ethics. It has to do with a patient whose initial claims represented the most elaborate and complex delusional system I've ever encountered. I was given express permission to tell the story in a public forum. Indeed, I was encouraged to do so.

Pathfinder

Most everyone could use a shrink now and again. We all have times in our lives when we could benefit from some support and direction from someone who, for the most part, is objective and outside the loop—an individual with the training and experience to help guide us through turbulent psychological waters.

There's no mystery as to why I think this way. I was trained formally and conservatively at fine schools, and in my practice I have prided myself in being a level-headed therapist. I have never trusted quick fixes or simplistic interpretations of complex human behavior. My organizing philosophy is to try to integrate and understand people from as many angles as possible. Viewing others on just one level of experience is hopelessly reductionistic. We are, of course, an amalgam of highly interrelational genetic, biologic, familial, and sociocultural factors. In point of fact, we are contextual psychological beings.

Becoming a seasoned guide wasn't just based on schooling and experience with patients. What I learned about others came in large measure from a deeper understanding of myself. I had been through my own challenges and dramas in life. I had stared into the mirror and analyzed everything from a thousand angles, sometimes with the help of my own therapist.

Individuals seeking treatment arrive for many reasons. People come to me for answers, often expecting that I can turn around a lifetime of dysfunction in less than an hour. Sometimes, I can't do that in a hundred hours. For the most part, patients want an epiphany. They're looking for an aha! moment where it all comes together in one sweeping instant—a nanosecond where confusion, self-doubt, and questioning disappear and their world at once becomes comprehensible.

Their hope is that they will stop feeling a sense of isolation and finally get what they believe others already have. They will no longer be looking from the outside in. Their body, mind, and spirit will come together in one dramatic understanding that goes beyond intellect and emotion.

For most of us, it won't play out like that. We'll spend our lives trying to sort out a huge puzzle by moving pieces about that sometimes fit and more often don't. In the end, we might discover that playing with the pieces was really just a way to occupy our minds.

I once estimated that I've spent some sixty thousand hours behind a closed door listening to people's problems. That doesn't include the hundreds of thousands of hours thinking about those problems. There really is no off duty when your mind is locked into the drama of other people's lives.

When prospective patients would ask me what I specialized in, I would think to myself, *I specialize in emotional pain and suffering,* though I settled for my stock phrase, which pretty much covered everything: "I deal in all types of intrapersonal and interpersonal issues."

I've heard about anxieties of all types: fears and worries that can sometimes paralyze, though more often they slowly bleed away the joy of life; imagined and real illnesses; despair leading to depression, where each day was a struggle just to get out of bed or to decide to stay alive.

There was an occasional suicide, followed by the ceaseless soul-searching that friends and family go through in trying to decide the what-if questions. I had been through such a gut-wrenching experience myself early in my career.

I was working the late-night shift at a psychiatric hospital while putting myself through medical school. One of the patients on my unit had been on suicide watch for a week. We had decided in staffing earlier that evening that he had improved enough to take him off of close observation. I don't recall the details of our last conversation together, but I do remember him going to bed and my wish that he "rest well."

Less than half an hour later, when doing my rounds, I found him hanging from a sheet tied to a pipe in the ceiling. I had sat a mere twenty feet away at the nursing station and not heard a sound. I can still clearly see him all these years later, slowly twirling around in a counterclockwise direction, and thinking how grotesque he looked. There was nothing peaceful about his death. It was violent and tragic.

I had tried to console parents who had lost a child through illness, drugs, war, or accident. Many times, I'd witnessed the devastating effects of substance abuse.

Certainly, people made each other crazy. Thousands of sessions involved relationship issues ranging from serious to trite. There were major crises involving domestic abuse, lying, and infidelity.

There were also squabbles where the couple bickered over the silliest matters. Spouses would badger each other, and I secretly visualized a tiny piranha gradually killing an elephant through not one bite, but a thousand.

Like any therapist, I have lots of war stories.

I once dismissed a patient by referring him out, once I realized he was an unrepentant pedophile under court-ordered treatment. On one occasion, I politely returned a pair of panties that flew across the room and neatly landed on my lap with an invitation to play.

I decided long ago in my career that I would try to listen well, offer encouragement, and firmly rest on the fact that I had very few definitive answers to many of life's trying events. Every person had a unique story and circumstance, and I had learned to believe that I could help the most by presuming the least.

At the same time, I quietly held the opinion that I had more or less heard it all. That's not to say I felt cocky or couldn't be humbled. Plenty of people reminded me that they would not act in a completely predictable way. Marriages survived when I was sure they'd fail. A lover would come back after a prolonged absence. Terminal cancer turned around. An endlessly relapsing drug addict, defying the odds, contacted me years later to let me know that he and his new family were doing great. There were many sad stories and successes as well.

Even so, after all these years, there wasn't anyone who was going to really challenge my understanding of the way our minds work. The numerators would certainly vary from person to person, but the basic psychological processes, the common denominators, were essentially the same. I felt with some certainty that, after thirty years of experience, I was pretty much a master mechanic practicing the art and soft social science of psychotherapy.

So when a new patient named Gabriel came in claiming to be God, I knew better than to throw his delusion back at him. Instead, I simply asked him how I, as a mere mortal, could be expected to offer help to the Supreme Being.

That one didn't throw Gabriel at all. He just smiled and replied, "Well, it turns out everyone can use a shrink. Even God."

Session One

. . . WAKE-UP CALL

Monday mornings are invariably busy for me, with lots of calls to return. There are new referrals and established patients who need appointments. I often hear from a couple who had a fight over the weekend, who have decided that they want to fix things once and for all, and could I get them in right away?

Or an alcoholic who left a message in the middle of the night about being done with drinking at last, ready to start life anew the very next morning. This is usually accompanied by the follow-up message that he is so sorry he called me while drunk and that he has forgotten what he said.

On this Monday morning, there wasn't

anything unusual about the last of the voice mails, either, although it was a stranger's voice.

"Hello, Dr. Johnson, this is Gabriel. I'd like to make an appointment. Please give me a call." His voice was soft, and he spoke clearly. His inflections were devoid of any particular accent. You can tell a lot about a new referral just from the tone of voice. Are they anxious? Depressed? Groggy? Eager to come in, or has someone put them up to it, as in an ultimatum: "Go see this guy or we're through!"

Gabriel's tone was pleasant enough, but it was also guarded. He wasn't letting any emotion through.

I recognized the prefix of his callback number. He was local.

"Hi, Gabriel. This is Dr. Johnson. You called for an appointment?"

"Yes. I'd like one as soon as you can get me in." I scanned my schedule.

"How about tomorrow morning at nine?"

"That's fine."

"Do you need directions?" I asked.

"I know how to get there."

"All right, how were you referred to me?"

He laughed out loud. "I know all about you."

His response caught me slightly off guard, but he said it in a friendly way.

"Okay, see you then."

~

On Tuesday morning, I arrived at my office fifteen minutes early. Just as every other day, I set the lighting, the music, and made sure everything was in perfect order. I had enough time to put on a small pot of coffee and check for last-minute messages.

My waiting room is designed to be psychologically disarming. From the moment someone walks in, they're greeted by soft lighting and warm, relaxing music that flows at just the right volume. The colors of the loveseat and two wingback chairs are neutral and pleasing to the eye. Magazines are escapist and have no connection to current events since I want patients to leave the rest of the world outside. To feel safe here. When they enter my office, an inner womb of sorts, they will be safer still.

There are no personal items of any sort in view. Nothing will distract them or give them explicit cause to wonder about my personal life. I dress in a casually professional manner. Sweaters are common, but never ties. Cologne is out of the question.

Nine o'clock arrived. Just as I began to think that Gabriel might be a no-show, the waiting room door opened and in he walked. We briefly exchanged greetings, then I showed him into my office and asked him to sit wherever he felt comfortable.

Shrinks are trained to analyze everything. The place he chose to sit would be worth noting. Most often, patients sit on the couch. I then take my place in a comfortable, over-stuffed chair across from them with a low coffee table in between. My diplomas hang strategically behind the chair to impart a sense of authority.

If a patient took my seat, it could be that the couch implied too much vulnerability for that person or perhaps that they wanted to be in a position of power.

Gabriel sat down in the middle of the sofa and began filling out the forms I'd given him.

"I'll be back in just a minute," I said. "Can I get you something?"

"Some of that coffee would be great if you have extra, black?"

"Sure."

Having him sit in the office for a couple of minutes by himself would give him a chance to absorb his new sur-roundings and collect his thoughts, since most people are nervous when they come to see a therapist.

Coffee in hand, I glanced over the intake form.

"What's your last name, Gabriel?"

"Let's just use my first name."

Looking further down, I was a bit surprised to see the

address left blank, as was the date of birth and the contact numbers. Under "occupation," it said "architect." I turned to the second page and saw that none of the other blanks had been filled in. Gabriel apparently had no family he wished to record nor any medical history. I kept a good poker face going and returned to the first page. Next to a line that read "reason for visit" was one word: "vent."

"I don't need your last name, though the other information would be helpful."

"It's not important."

I nodded, but my wheels started spinning. Was he a criminal? A psychotic? Probably just a wiseass. If he was, this was early to be positioning for power. Whatever the reason, he wasn't about to derail me.

"That's fine." It wasn't fine. I pushed on.

"You're an architect?"

"Yes."

"With a firm?" Like he was about to tell me.

"No. I work with very complex systems."

"Like bridges, buildings?" I asked, grasping for an anchor.

Gabriel smiled broadly, a warm and friendly smile. With a kind face and simple features, he could easily walk down the street unnoticed. Nothing in his dress or appearance stood out. He was of average height and weight and looked to be somewhere in his thirties, though his paperwork wasn't helping me any.

"No. The systems I work with are more complex than that."

"Artificial intelligence." I said that with assurance, suddenly pleased with myself that I'd figured it out.

Gabriel's face turned serious.

"I chose *you*, Doc."

"I know that, but I still don't know how you were referred to me."

For a split second, I thought he looked exasperated.

"No. *I chose you*." He paused for a moment, then added, "You may want to trade places with me and sit on the couch. This is going to be hard to understand."

I felt my heart start to race and a bead of sweat formed on my forehead. Great way to start the day. I had a disquieting feeling and took a long, deep breath. I suddenly felt like I was losing control of the session, and that is something I never let happen.

"Listen, Gabriel, let's rewind the tape. What brings you here?"

"I'm God, and I'm here to vent."

I fell silent. At least things were clearer now. I was dealing with a psychotic. I had no idea what the particulars of his delusional system were yet, but I was fairly certain it was some type of paranoid state, or maybe paranoid schizophrenia. I'd had a lot of experience working with psychotics, particularly earlier in my career, so I immediately felt calmer.

The game plan crystallized in my mind like a well-worn habit. I'd be very gentle but firm with him and make an appropriate referral to a colleague more specialized in treating seriously mentally ill patients.

"Are you on any medication, Gabriel?" I asked in an assertive tone.

He smiled a knowing smile.

"I'm going to prove it to you, Doctor."

What was this guy going to do? A scary scene from my past flashed through my mind. A distraught patient had once pulled a gun out of his briefcase without first making it clear that he was only bringing it to me for safekeeping. I will never forget that moment of sheer terror while I quickly weighed options. Was he going to shoot himself in front of me—or kill me first? I could only hope that he would just say some crazy things and let it go at that.

"I'm not going to do tricks," he said firmly. "How about if I just read your mind?"

Great, I thought, *a psychic psychotic.*

"You got up this morning at precisely 7:31. You had two dreams, the one you remember about your vacation in Cancun and the one you don't about drowning in a pool. You took an aspirin for your hangover, obsessed about being fat, weighed yourself three times, and told yourself you'd jog after work and listen to Fleetwood Mac on your iPod.

"You wondered if your hair was receding and if you had bad breath. You thought about the day ahead and looked over at the bed wishing you could climb back in. You promised to stop being so hard on yourself but thought you'd die that way. I'm leaving out the weird stuff because I don't want to embarrass you. By the way, Richard, I'm not a psychotic who thinks he's psychic."

I sat speechless for a few seconds, looking for some kind of explanation. He could be a stalker, but the information was too detailed. The only rational explanation was that this man calling himself Gabriel actually was a psychic. I once had a patient who had also appeared to demonstrate true psychic abilities, so it was possible, and I had always been open to that possibility in certain people.

"When you were seven years old, on a hot Wednesday, July 27, 1960, your grandfather was visiting from North Carolina and you begged him to go fishing. You idolized him for good reason. He was a kind man. You caught three fish and on the way home, your bucket fell to the ground and one of them jumped back into the canal. Then you began crying and your grandfather took you back and you fished for what seemed like hours until he caught another one. You still speak to him privately in your mind, mostly at night when you can't sleep. There's this secret promise you made to yourself years ago to go visit his grave, although you never have. Don't try to figure this out. Just accept it."

I had all but forgotten that story. What he'd said happened so fast that I had trouble absorbing it. Still, even if he could read my mind with perfect accuracy all day long, he was still claiming to be God. My questions came out like a reflex.

"Okay. Why does God need to vent? And why would he want to talk to me? I'm hardly the most qualified."

"You're qualified enough. That's why I chose you."

"Why me?"

"A few reasons. You're a good listener and bound to confidentiality." He smiled broadly again.

"You also realize you don't know much. That's a compliment, not a criticism."

Despite the situation, the anxiety I had felt before was now gone. I sank deeper into my chair dumbfounded. He was capable of being charismatic, which necessitated action on my part. I would have to be careful not to be drawn into a false sense of comfort and risk being disarmed.

"I took your fear away. It doesn't help me to have you so tense. After all, you're going to be my therapist."

There's a point in time in which a therapist can challenge a delusional system or simply enter into it in an observing way. The tighter the delusions are, the more systematized and elaborate, the less value in a direct confrontation. At this early point in Gabe's therapy, it would be wiser to play along. In that way, I would be more likely to develop a trusting relationship from which I could gently dismantle his psychosis.

"I can't guide God," I said.

"I'm not looking for advice. I'm here to vent, remember?"

"To vent . . . ?"

"Richard, I don't want to spend much more time on this. Belief or lack thereof is your issue. We're burning off my time."

Wanting to play along, I said, "What could God possibly need to talk about?"

"A great many things," he answered.

"So let's see if I've got this right: I'm going to be God's shrink?"

"You already are."

Before I could respond he explained, "I'll see you once a week for a session, and I get to talk about anything I want. You can listen and ask questions, but I don't need any advice."

"Oh, well, hey. That's a relief—I don't need to give God advice." I couldn't help grinning.

"There are two rules, Richard. The first one is don't ask the questions you know not to ask, and second, you have to respect my confidentiality. Is that agreed?"

"Agreed. But Gabriel, it's only fair to tell you that I would willingly agree to those terms with any patient."

"One more thing, from this point on, call me Gabe."

I repeated my agreement to all of his terms, after again pointing out that his requirements were no more than those I always extend in my work. He didn't pay any attention to that the second time, either.

That first session ended with Gabe reaching into his pocket and producing the exact amount of cash to pay for the visit. The bills were crisp and newly minted.

"You didn't think God would ask for special favors, did you?" he asked.

Yes, a definite psychotic; maybe even a serial killer. It was only ten o'clock and I found myself thinking that I should have been a lawyer like my brother.

Session Two

. . . A REGULAR GUY

You don't have to be trained as a therapist to analyze things from a psychological point of view. Yet, for me, it is an inevitable occupational hazard. I always found myself thinking about the underlying meaning of what everyone said and did. But now that I've been doing this work for some time, listening with the "third ear" is a natural occurrence, personally and professionally.

I've always lived in a world of thought and reflection; my own neurotic issues provided another layer of mental challenge. There were my obsessive-compulsive traits to contend with, as well as my tendency to be overly self-critical. A recent breakup with my girlfriend of six months once again seemed to prove to me that I couldn't sustain an intimate relationship with anyone for any length of time. She had described me as "overly analytical and emotionally detached." While my professional life involved the encouragement of healthy human connections, my personal life was one of relative isolation. There were times when I felt like a fraud.

With Gabe, I felt certain that any serious attempt to analyze the meaning behind what he was saying to me would be futile. I didn't have any context to work from and couldn't help but wonder, *Did he have friends? A family? A job?*

I felt challenged, I admit, and a little exhilarated with the opportunity Gabe had given me. His razor-sharp psychic abilities captured my full attention and represented a potential break from the usual stories of the walking wounded.

On the morning of our second session, I had one appointment before his.

Maureen was my pro bono case. I had seen her on and off for over ten years and witnessed many trials in her life. She would call for an appointment or two, and then I might not see her for months at a time. She would resurface when she encountered a problem with her mentally handicapped son or needed advice on some romantic matter.

Today she came to me with an appeal to help her reconnect with her estranged daughter. They hadn't been in contact for over three years because of a falling out over some man she'd been dating. Maureen said that he was a loser, and that was that.

I devised a simple plan to write a letter on Maureen's behalf. In it, I would explain the reason for my letter and ask that her daughter consider contacting me so that I might act as an intermediary in the hopes of reconnecting them. Since her daughter had been a patient of mine, years ago when she was an adolescent, and I'd had a good relationship with her, I thought we had a fairly good chance. The letter would be sent to her last-known address.

When Gabe's appointment time arrived, I fought the urge to peer out the window down to the parking lot out of a sense of anticipation at diving into this interesting new case. I eventually gave into temptation, but I saw no car arrive, even though the office window has a commanding view of the parking lot.

At precisely 9:00 AM, the door to my waiting room opened.

In addition to the details I took in during our first meeting, I now doubled my efforts. His clothes, gait, and nonverbal gestures were inventoried for some kind of a clue as to who he really was. But as I scrutinized him, it dawned on me that there wasn't anything in particular that stood out about him. He came across as a real *Everyman*. Tough guy to pick out of a police lineup. I hoped that I wouldn't have to, but with delusional patients, you never know for sure which direction their symptoms will turn in, or when.

I pushed back the desire to pepper him with questions. Keeping one's own thoughts and feelings in check is a prerequisite to being an effective therapist. Using one's own reactions as an index of how to help someone is fine, but therapy is for the patient, not the therapist.

We both took a seat.

"What troubles you the most?" It was a simple, leading, clichéd, and open-ended question. Almost all therapy patients end up talking about the real reason they came into therapy. The presenting problem is seldom the real one. Gabriel closed his eyes and thought deeply, as he would so many times in the weeks to come.

"People think and believe I'm perfect. That I'm this all-knowing, wise creator of the universe who can do anything he wants."

"And that's not true?"

"That's not what I am in reality, Richard, but it's the way everyone wants to see me."

"So who are you really?"

"In many ways, I'm a regular guy."

"It's hardly possible for God to be a regular guy," I responded.

"I've got problems just like everyone else."

"That's quite a shift in conventional thinking," I said. "Everyone thinks that God's flawless."

"That's ridiculous. The universe is perfect and imperfect at the same time. Why shouldn't that hold true with me? The problem is that people don't care to live in a paradox. They feel more secure with clear answers."

"What are your issues, then?"

"That's going to become clearer to you." He waved his hand. "It's true that I did put all of this in motion. But I'm not responsible for everything that's happened since. That's where people and free will come in.

"As for me, I never get angry or vengeful or any of that. I have a great capacity for love and compassion, but it comes at a price to me. I'm emotionally exhausted at times. I get worn down and frustrated by lots of things."

"That's another revelation, then." I took care not to sound sarcastic. "I've never heard anyone consider God to be capable of wearing down. What frustrates you the most?"

"Stupidity is probably at the top of my list. It's at the heart of nearly every conflict, and yet so much conflict is really nonsense."

"You mean conflict between individuals or nations?"

"Choice C, both of the above."

"You know, I can't help asking you this." I paused for a second. "If you created the universe, did you create such a flawed system on purpose?"

"No. It's not working out quite the way I envisioned. We're in pretty deep. Consider it a work in progress."

Gabe scanned the room and focused his gaze on a small figure of African carved art.

"I'm not the creator, I'm the producer. The architect."

"What does that mean?" I asked.

"I put all the pieces together in one place. I gathered all the resources, but I have limited control over how everything is unfolding. Each person is really the director of their own story." He paused a moment and quickly added, "That's if the person is blessed with the privilege of choice. Many people don't have any."

"Doesn't everyone have *some* degree of free will?"

"No. There are a great many people whose life paths are completely determined by what they're born with, physically and mentally, where and to whom. Many millions are trapped by poverty, disease, and despair. Their options are determined by outside forces. The privileged classes labor under the delusion that everyone has the ability to rise above their circumstances."

That's an interesting twist, I thought to myself, a psychotic patient referring to others as delusional.

"So who created the universe?"

"That's one of the questions you shouldn't ask of me. I get frustrated with it myself. The truth is, I don't know who or what created the material world."

So God doesn't have all the answers? I thought. "I don't mean any disrespect, Gabe, but how could you really be God if you aren't the ultimate creator?"

"What makes anyone think there's one creator? I'm fine with unknowns. Unanswered questions aren't a problem, and the mystery doesn't bother me."

"What else tires you?" I asked.

"Before I answer that, let me explain something. There absolutely is a spiritual, nonmaterial side to life. There's no need to prove or disprove that. Most people recognize that intuitively, even if they may intellectually deny it. A crisis of faith is an altogether different issue. For now, just follow me on this spiritual track, okay?"

"Okay."

"I have many billions of lives to track. People who've lived before, those who are alive today, and those to come. When things are going well, the work is easier. But whose life is a static condition of bliss? I'm burdened a lot. I'm burned out sometimes."

"Are you aware of every detail in everyone's life?"

"I am if I decide to focus on something or if a detail

comes to my attention. Otherwise, I don't track every little bit of minutiae. I pay more attention to the bigger events, especially those that dramatically alter someone's life, either physically or spiritually. At the same time, there's a relativity to people's lives, isn't there? You know that too well with what you do. How many people come in to see you and say 'I know other people have it far worse than I do, and my life is blessed compared to others, but . . .'"

He was right, of course. I had learned long ago that when someone says "but" in the middle of an explanation, it means that what's being said next is what they really care about.

"Sometimes," I agreed.

"People are the center of their own experience. That's the way it is. It's a built-in egocentric perspective and experience of life. It's not good or bad. It's the way things are. We're all intricately bound, and yet separate. Another paradox."

"Let's get back to you, Gabe."

"Like I said, I get tired. Problems wear me down."

"How do you get recharged?" I asked.

"I get recharged in a couple of ways. Through the natural world, and by observing the good in people. I'm extremely interested in how each person uses their individual gifts. Everyone has unique talents. The expression of those talents in actions that help or enrich the lives of others is pleasing to me. The truth is that I get frustrated by unnecessary suffering on a larger scale."

He fixed his eyes directly on mine and asked, "You know what really bothers me?"

"What?" I asked.

"Poor or misdirected leadership. People in a position of power have tremendous influence over the lives of others."

"That sounds political."

"If you think of politics as the will of a few people directing the masses, which is what it is, then I'm political."

This subject was worth spending some time on. Many psychotics begin to ramble when talking about religion or politics. Within that rambling there might be a key.

"Who's to judge what good or poor leadership is? Doesn't it depend on what your beliefs are?" I queried.

"*Everything* titrates down to what your beliefs are. What one values is either taught or acquired. Many people think for themselves, but what they consider the raw materials of thought are processed before general consumption. The real leaders, especially in the age you're living in, Richard, are the gatekeepers of information."

"What does that mean?"

"What one is fed they will digest. It turns out that great

leadership promotes the good of humanity, and poor leadership is a function of misaligned values or incompetence."

"Who determines what's best?"

"You and every single person who is able to. Change has to happen on a micro level first. It gains momentum, and then, before you know it, we take a step forward or backward. Look, Richard, much of reality is simply a matter of consensus. We generally agree that something is this or that.

"Political power is the ability to influence someone to do something they otherwise wouldn't necessarily do on their own accord. And politics isn't about ideas only. Ultimately, it changes the way the world, or a part of it at least, is experienced. With all the intelligence present in the world at any given time, it's disturbing to look at some individuals in major positions of power."

For the first time, I could detect a slight agitation in his voice. I'd been waiting for this, because so far Gabe sounded too analytical. The emotions behind the words had been missing, up to this point. I wasn't too thrilled about doing this, but I decided to prod him on a bit.

"You sound angry."

"More like frustrated."

"Would it be all right if you *were* angry?" I asked.

"Richard, I know how this game is played," he said with a grin. "Besides, our time's up today."

Session Three

. . . THE FLOOD GATES

By the second session, I typically have the feeling that I've known the patient for a long time. I can readily identify with the issue at hand either from a personal experience standpoint or a recognition that I'd seen it before.

That wasn't the case with Gabriel. I couldn't relate to his grandiose ideas about being God. While many of the things he'd said and done so far were interesting, they were the product of a deeply disturbed individual. I was eager to have my session with Gabe but there were two appointments ahead of him.

If being a victim could be a profession, then Paul would no doubt have a great career. The world was, according to his version of it, always conspiring against him. Nothing ever went his way, and everyone was either incompetent or just plain stupid. I usually just listened to him and never tried very hard to help him see the self-defeating patterns of his life.

As far as he was concerned, I was perhaps the only person who had ever been in his corner. I wasn't entirely sure if my passive listening to him, peppered with occasional supportive comments, was what he needed, or what I needed because it was just easier that way.

Today was no different. He registered a litany of complaints and went on his way relieved that he'd dumped on someone willing to listen.

My second patient had some serious concerns. Marty's most recent counts indicated that his HIV was in check. He was going through a tough time with his current lover, who wasn't sure he could cope with the "complication" of dating someone with the virus. Marty didn't blame him for feeling that way. He was struggling with the disappointment of another failed relationship. His anxiety was almost crippling at times, and he looked to me as if I might have the power to take it all away. I upped his dose of diazepam and told him I'd see him next week. Now I could focus on Gabe…

Diagnostically, I believed that I was dealing with a paranoid psychosis. I wasn't able to differentiate much further than that since he wasn't interested in giving me any history. The delusional system seemed to be tightly woven and elaborate. His thinking wasn't disorganized, and his affect, while slightly blunted, wasn't inappropriate. If he didn't talk about his crazy ideas, he could readily pass through life with an otherwise undetected mental illness.

Once again, the door to the waiting room opened at precisely the right time. I had a cup of coffee waiting, which he accepted eagerly.

"How are you?" I asked.

"I'm burdened. I'll even admit that I can get depressed sometimes."

"Depressed?"

"Overwhelmed might be a better word. Doc, my name is called out several billion times a day in joy, sorrow, anger, desperation, confusion, and prayer. And I do hear it every time."

"You don't act on everything." That was said more as an observation than a challenge. I quickly filed away the word "depressed."

"Listening is exhausting, and the truth is I can't act on everything. That's why there's suffering in the world. I simply don't control all of it. People don't understand that. There are forces in motion beyond me. And, like I said last week, there's free will."

This was one of those strategic points where the therapist is wise to keep quiet for the moment. The simple asking of a question, either prematurely or one that directs the therapy along a different path, can inadvertently cut-off a patient's train of thought.

"I'm deeply sorrowful about people's suffering," he continued. "It's everywhere."

I let that sit in the air for awhile.

"So how do you view yourself?" I finally asked.

"A focal point. I'm an organizing force for people's beliefs."

He paused for a moment before continuing.

"Look at it this way, Richard. You know those inkblots that used to be popular in your work?"

"Of course," I answered. He was referring to the Rorschach test that consists of inkblots that are interpreted according to a person's distinct perceptions.

"I'm like one of those cards. Many people see me a certain way because they've been taught to or perhaps even coerced. Others have a self-created view of me that's more unique. The interpretation changes, but the substance of who I am remains stable. The truth is, I don't really care how people view me so long as they don't claim exclusive rights to knowing who I am. I want a perception of me that encourages love and goodness. And what's a good person? That's common sense."

"Do you want prayer and worship?" I asked.

"Not the way most people think of it. Although welcomed because it reinforces a connection to me, I don't need millions of repetitions of the same words to get my attention. I already know the prayers. I do like the focus that goes along with prayer. The intent behind it. The idea that someone is communing with a force bigger than themselves that is also within them. I'm not out there, Richard. I'm in here." He pressed his hand over his heart.

I could tell he was on a roll.

"And worship? That makes me a little nuts. I don't have this ego that requires constant feeding. Gratitude and appreciation for whatever blessings we have in life are great. I love humility but not self-deprecation. I don't like the idea that I am a superior being that people are unworthy to be in the presence of. If someone feels better bowing and kneeling, that's their choice. I don't need it. I'm not needy and insecure."

I found that last point especially intriguing. Grandiose delusional systems are typically characterized by fantasies of great power, fame, or wealth. Humility is not associated with an inflated sense of self. On the other hand, Gabe *was* claiming to be God. One can't get any more over the top than that.

"Where does spiritual suffering come from?"

"Mostly from the confusion and doubt that come with

physical and emotional pain. I'm expected to solve everything."

"Doesn't religion seek to clear that up?"

"Religion is mixed for me. On one hand, it can separate people and place boundaries on experience. On the other hand, it's often a blueprint for proper action."

I was very curious as to which way he was going to go on this.

"There are many fine religions, but I never liked the idea that one path should be followed to the exclusion of others. To tell you the truth, what people do is far more important to me than what they think."

He hesitated a moment.

"Since you're my shrink, I can tell you everything." That was expressed as a statement, not a question.

"Absolutely."

"I see the enormous value in religion for a lot of people. If it's understood properly, it encourages them to live on a higher plane. At the very same time, though, I'm much more pleased with atheists who devote their whole lives to relief work than a person who claims to be religious but doesn't do anything meaningful for others."

Gabe was becoming more focused.

"It's really not that complicated. I get frustrated with anyone who thinks they have a corner on the spiritual market."

There was something disturbing in what Gabe was saying. Religious delusions are almost invariably dogmatic and fixed, or they're hopelessly disorganized. The articulations of his beliefs were anything but. He had clearly spent time reflecting on these issues. Were it not for the fact that he was claiming he was God, Gabe could readily pass off his beliefs as global philosophical concepts.

Still, he believed that he was carrying the burden of the world's sufferings on his own shoulders, which was an enormous psychological strain. Gabe wasn't falling as neatly into the diagnostic category as I had earlier thought. I'd change my working diagnosis to "atypical psychosis."

"Different religions are all roads that lead to the same place. The destination is the origin of everything. You've heard this a million times because it's true. The road loops back on itself, and in that sense, life is a circle."

"Gabriel is a Hebrew name." I pointed out the obvious.

"Right. An archangel and a messenger. I used it for convenience. Don't overinterpret everything," he said with a smile.

I had to admit to myself that I liked hearing all of this because it fit in with my own views. I'd grown up in a Catholic family and been confused for some time about religious matters. I'd even occasionally attended the Unitarian Fellowship, a spiritual refuge camp of sorts, but eventually returned to my Catholic roots. I enjoyed the traditions, though I felt strangely detached from them. I'd look around church every Sunday and think that everyone else understood except for me.

It was the part about submission and surrendering that was hard for me. I was sure that God wanted us to think for ourselves.

I approached religion more from a perspective of respect. That made sense to me. I believed strongly in God and knew in my own life that I'd received many blessings. I was convinced that God had seen me through many difficult times, so a faith in God's existence was never an issue for me. I just accepted that I didn't know much about how it all worked.

"You know, Richard, I don't understand a lot of things about religion myself." Gabe said in a perplexed tone. "The details get very esoteric."

"How could God get confused about religion?"

"Easily. There are some amazing traditions and interpretations, although many have been filtered and reprocessed. So much of what is really simple has been made complicated. The fundamentals of what it takes to be a good person aren't rocket science. It's basically common sense. Just pay attention to the goodness in each other. There's an immediate recognition of what goodness is."

"Does everything happen for a reason?"

"There's some great choreography going on, so yes,

lots of things fit into a bigger scheme. There are random events, too. When someone tragically dies for no reason, a lot of people cry out that it's God's will. Let me tell you something. It's not my will."

"Doesn't God see what's up ahead?" I asked.

"Like *your* death, Richard? How and when you'll die?"

I sat there motionless. It was tempting, but I really did not want to know the answer to that particular question. Whether or not he actually had any predictive psychic abilities or not wasn't the issue. Knowing myself, I'd be unable to put the date aside and end up obsessing about it. In any event, it was surely one of those questions I shouldn't be asking.

"I know *everything* about your life. It's like watching a movie you produced. Sort of like an independent film. If I decide to watch it, I'll know how it ends even as you're still filming it. This much I can tell you: at the instant of your death, everything becomes crystal clear. It all makes immediate sense."

"That sounds vague and mysterious," I finally said.

"Exactly. It's all confounding. Nothing goes unnoticed, and life is a training ground . . . in part."

"For what?"

"Everyone needs to work on their own evolution while they're here. Their personal development will add or subtract from everyone else's. Did your presence here move humanity forward or backward? That's up to each person to answer for themselves."

Gabe seemed to be an enigma.

"Puzzling, isn't it?" he asked.

"Very," I answered.

"Good. I really don't care for anyone who thinks they have all the answers to everything. The world is full of puzzles. At the same time, the natural order of things is pretty straightforward. The desire to control creates complication out of simplicity. What many would call primitive, I would consider natural."

Gabe looked me over as though he were studying me.

"What do you think makes a good teacher?" he asked me.

"Having the right answers," I responded.

"More often it's knowing the right questions."

He had no watch on, but somehow he knew that precisely fifty minutes had passed.

"We can go over today, Gabe. I have the time."

"See you next week, Doc," he said as he stood up to leave.

I was unsatisfied with the intellectual tone of the session. I sensed that there was much more about his emotional life than he let on. Hadn't he used the word "depressed" in describing himself? What did he mean when he'd said in an earlier session that things hadn't turned out as planned and that "we're in too deep"?

Gabe was in trouble, and he needed more than just a place to vent. He was suffering, and it was my responsibility to root out the source of that pain. It didn't seem to be simply a question of a chemical imbalance or a genetic anomaly. His delusions were more complicated than that.

The problem was that, on a broader scale, I found that what he was saying made sense to me. Sane views coming from an insane man.

Something else tugged at my mind. All of my patients are invariably engrossed with some aspect of their own lives. Gabe was preoccupied with everyone else's welfare.

Hopefully, I could eliminate this delusion or at least get him to the point where his misjudged belief didn't cause him to suffer anymore.

Session Four

. . . CRITICAL MASS

Gabe was very intriguing, to say the least, but I had other patients to attend to—specifically, three other sessions to consider before I'd meet with him. I would do my best to focus on their needs, but given the inherent interesting nature of Gabe's case, that would be hard to do.

Elaine snorted a few lines of cocaine over the weekend, but otherwise felt that her recovery was going pretty well. She thought the ninety-meetings-in-ninety-days recommendation that had been made during her recent inpatient treatment was too much to ask of her. Elaine said she could not relate to the other addicts. The meetings she'd gone to while an inpatient were okay, but now that she was out, she believed she could handle things on her own.

I mapped out a plan for her designed to maximize her chances of success, but reminded her that the power of any addiction is in its ability to get fed by being resourceful and creative.

Brian came in next and wanted a session of hypnosis to help him get over his driving phobia. Side roads were fine, but he hadn't been on the interstate in over five years. Not once. Considering that he was in sales and needed to drive to many appointments, he figured his avoidance behavior tacked on at least another fifteen hours a week to his driving. Like most people with phobias, he knew his fears were exaggerated and somewhat irrational.

Brian was a good subject, and I made the suggestion under hypnosis that he would be able to drive one exit with a complete sense of control and relaxation. I then told him that he should feel free to accept or reject the suggestion but that he should immediately get on the highway after our session and make that decision *right after* he exited.

I told him to trust that his mind wouldn't allow him to be put in a truly risky situation. An hour later, he called me on his cell phone in almost a euphoric state to let me know he had driven straight to the highway after our appointment and was doing great. Brian's phobia, and its apparently simple resolution, gave me a sense of satisfaction. It wasn't often that I had a linear solution to a problem.

My third patient, Louis, was a living storybook example of devoted love. His wife of over fifty years had developed a rapidly progressing dementia. There were times when she couldn't even recognize him anymore.

Louis had himself suffered a stroke recently and walked with some difficulty. His mental functioning was entirely intact. He resisted his children's push that he move their mother into a nursing home, insisting that he could and would care for her.

Like clockwork, he came to see me every other week. In all honesty, I couldn't describe these appointments as therapy in the traditional sense. Louis would simply share a cup of coffee with me and converse for an hour about anything that occurred to him. He particularly enjoyed telling me stories from his past. Whenever I'd ask how things were going at home, he'd dismiss his trials there in a matter-of-fact manner and move on to something else. I never pushed it, and he never complained.

It was time to turn my attention to Gabe. During the week that passed, I had fortified my resolve to steer away from questions that were really geared toward my need to have my curiosity satisfied. In retrospect, I found that my line of questioning had been somewhat self-serving. Gabe was one of the most interesting patients I'd had in my career. I would have to control my inclination to explore his psychological architecture in any fashion other than what was expressly geared toward helping him. I decided it was time to carefully dismantle his defenses and find out what was really going on inside.

The first step was to use one of his own delusions to our mutual advantage.

"Do you know what I'm thinking at all times?" I asked as we settled in.

"Like I said last time, if I want to. But I'm not focusing on you, Richard, so the short answer is no. I don't want to be on duty in here."

"Good. Because I *am* on duty. You and I have some work to do," I said in a self-assured tone.

I wasn't certain if the look on his face was one of surprise or if he'd expected this.

"I know that you might not be thrilled with this, but I need to ask you some more structured questions."

"You mean a mental status examination."

"You've had one before?"

"No. It's a waste of time, but if it makes you feel better, go ahead and give it to me."

There were many elements of the examination that I'd already noted. His clothing remained plain. He always wore a simple white shirt and black slacks. No watch or jewelry of any sort. Attention to personal hygiene was normal.

Gabe's eye contact was appropriate. I hadn't noticed any mannerisms whatsoever so far that would reveal an element of character. That in itself was highly unusual in that everyone has a particular set of habits that are quickly revealed in the first few sessions. Since most are unconscious and ingrained, it's virtually impossible to hide all of them.

He was entirely relaxed. While he was personable enough, I couldn't say that he was entirely cooperative in that he wouldn't share basic background information about himself. Gabe had tried to take control of the therapy from the very beginning. I couldn't rule out the possibility that he might have oppositional or perhaps passive-aggressive personality traits.

So far, his range of emotions had been somewhat restricted and guarded. His mood was a mixture of neutral and pleasant.

With respect to delusions, that was self-evident. He was convinced that he was God.

The time had come to gather information I couldn't infer. It would help to establish myself as the doctor and he the patient. It would also implicitly reinforce the idea that there was something mentally wrong with him.

"Do you hear voices, Gabe?"

"Billions."

"From the same source or different ones?"

"Every single person on the planet. Let's move on, Richard. You're not ready to tackle this one yet." He said that firmly.

"What do those voices say?"

"Everything you can imagine and everything you can't."

"That sounds cryptic," I said. "Can you be more specific?"

"No, I can't. Let's move on."

"Do you sometimes see things others can't?" I asked a little more firmly.

"Of course. I don't even want to try and explain that to you. Suffice it to say that I see everything all the time."

"Do you think that you have problems?"

"Yes. That's one of the reasons I'm here."

"What kind of problems?"

"That will become clear as you get to know me."

I wasn't able to assess his insight any further than these few questions. Capacity for judgment is typically evaluated from history or perhaps collateral sources like family or friends. That wasn't going to happen.

"Can you repeat some numbers back to me?"

"Sure. We can start out slow or take it to the end and save some time. How about you give me a string of twenty-five randomly chosen single digits and I'll say them backward for you or in any order you desire. Square roots? It doesn't matter to me."

"Single digits will be fine."

I thought he was being smart with me until he progressively repeated all twenty-five digits flawlessly *backward*. That was impressive in its own right, but the part that really astonished me was that he thought it might be amusing if he took any number I picked at random and multiplied it by the remaining twenty-four *simultaneously*. I wrote those astronomical figures down and used a calculator to determine he was right every time.

The fact that he was a mathematical wizard didn't prove he was God. I moved on to memory.

"I'm going to repeat three words that I'd like you to remember. Later on I'll be asking you to recall them. The words are 'tree,' 'pear,' and 'chair.'"

Gabe seemed to look through me. Maybe he thought I was the stupidest man he'd ever met. After his mathematical demonstration, I felt a little foolish myself in asking these questions, but I was determined.

"How about you make up a story about your tree, pear, and a chair, and I'll remember all of it anytime you desire?"

That was a highly unusual request, but it came from an extraordinarily unusual patient. I had to think fast on my feet. I decided to go with it.

"A seventy-five-year-old man with a burning hunger stood six feet tall. On a hot day, he walked by a pear tree and spying a pear beyond his reach, searched for a way to get it. An old brown chair lay nearby, and he stood on it. Biting into the fruit, he savored the taste and his good fortune."

"Not bad, Richard."

"Why should people in glass houses not throw stones?" I continued.

"A concrete answer would be so they don't break the glass. A more abstract response would be that we should be careful not to criticize others as we have our own faults. I like that proverb."

I was going to test his general fund of knowledge next. If his knowledge base was anything like his mathematical ability, I would need to come up with something esoteric.

"Which city has the most crime in the world?"

"Somewhat ironically, it's the Vatican. There's more crime there per capita, in excess of twenty times that of the rest of Italy, than anywhere else in the world. The statistic is a little misleading, though, considering that the Vatican is really a city-state with a small resident population and millions of visitors."

I couldn't help feeling a little foolish at this point.

"Do you have any thoughts about hurting yourself or others?"

"No."

He was passing the examination with flying colors.

"Why did you *really* come to see me, Gabe?" I asked.

"I came to talk."

"About what really? That you're having a tough time with us? Why would now be any different than any other time in history or in the future?" I said this with a very slight air of provocation. These were exploratory questions designed to give him a push forward, to say something he might not otherwise say. Before he could answer, another question popped into my mind.

"Is this the first time you've talked to a therapist?"

"Yes."

"Why now?"

"Because I'm on the edge."

"The edge of what?"

He stopped for a moment as if to deliberate whether or not he was going to tell me.

"I'm running out of energy. I'm tired, and the world is getting more complex than ever." Then he looked me squarely in the eye. "You want to know why I *really* came to see you?"

"Of course I do." I felt like a skater on a winter's pond,

testing the thickness of the ice, unsure of where the thin part was, pushing on anyway.

"I feel helpless sometimes."

For the first time I noticed a change in his tone. He was saddened. Were we getting closer to something?

"Everyone expects me to be perfect. I don't have all the answers, and I can't save everyone. I have limits. Can you understand that?"

I shrugged my shoulders slightly. This was his ball game.

"I'll let you in on a little secret, Richard. Humans *are* made in my image, so why wouldn't I have some of the same problems? It turns out that the architect didn't have a flawless design."

"But you said in our last session that you didn't create the universe," I asked with some challenge in my tone.

"The manifestation of raw materials isn't of interest to me. It's the totally unique way in which I put them together that's my domain."

I needed to push this along a little further. Most psychotics begin to sweat when they're painted into a logical corner.

"Gabe, wouldn't God know that *he* created the universe?"

"Maybe, if we were dealing with a monotheistic system. Since we're not, that doesn't apply to me."

"You're trying to tell me there's more than one God?"

"I'm telling you there is more than one interpretation of me. Can I continue?"

I wasn't completely satisfied with that answer, but part of me realized immediately that I had to be careful not to fall into a trap. Since the subject matter interested me, I would have to guard against the subtle shift from a therapy session to an interview.

"Of course you can," I said.

"The truth is, I put something in motion that I couldn't completely predict."

"What can you do about it?" I asked.

"That's not the right question. It would be more proper to ask what it is that people can do about it. Believing that the world is a fragile place is a truism."

"Isn't life always fragile?"

"Not like this. Everything is converging in a way that it never has before—both for good and bad."

"Good and evil?"

That last question was a setup. I was trying to bait him a bit. If I could get him to admit that he was predicting an apocalyptic showdown between the forces of good and evil, I could readily understand his grandiosity in the service of a delusion that Gabe's mission was to save the world from itself. In that way, I could tie up my understanding of him and plan my intervention accordingly.

"People would be naive to think that there aren't forces

at work within an individual or on the world at large."

"Aren't conflicts inevitable?"

"No, they're not," he answered without hesitation. "It's much more complicated than a simple showdown between good and evil. Think about this, Richard. For the very first time in history, all of the resources are available to those who have the power to put them to good use. Whether it's a national or an individual effort, there's a lot that can be done. Free will and the ability to change the world are present at the same time. How's that for a combination? Life can be improved dramatically for those who hunger."

"Hunger for what?" I asked.

"Anything and everything. Food, medicine, knowledge, faith. Any kind of resource can be shifted to where it's needed the most."

"That seems simplistic."

"That's right," Gabe replied. "The solution *is* simple, and the implementation is a question of logistics."

"So what prevents that from happening more often?"

"Mostly ignorance, fear, and greed. Nothing new really. It's just that those forces can easily tip the balance."

"So where does that leave you, Gabe?"

He thought that question over for a moment.

"At a breaking point," he answered.

"What does that mean?" I asked.

"I'm chronically stressed. War, poverty, illnesses—these relentless burdens are weighing me down. The pressures are intense. It's time for a lot of people to grow up and stop being so self-absorbed."

"Grow up?"

"Overall, the evolution of humanity is a very slow burn, and immaturity frustrates me." For just a split second, I thought I saw a deep exhaustion behind his eyes.

"Are you giving up on us, Gabe?" The question imbedded behind this was a query into whether he was giving up on himself. He was projecting all over the place.

"No. It's not like that." He paused, and I could sense a shift in his thinking. "This whole debate about evolution or creationism is interesting but misses the point, don't you think?"

"What do you mean?" I asked, unsure of where he was going.

"There's a spiritual evolution that's lagging behind the needs of the world. Think of it as a resource that's being outstripped by the demand. Scarcity of oil isn't going to be the problem, the shortage of genuine compassion is."

The simple interpretations of his delusions had escaped me once again. Our conversation was flirting on the edge of something deeper, though I couldn't tell just what. I steadfastly hung on to the belief that there was a major revelation about Gabe's nature that was right in front of me. It wouldn't come from something he said, but there was a clue hiding somewhere between the lines that would take me to the next level.

"We're almost out of time, Richard," Gabe said.

Suddenly and inexplicably, I became convinced that I'd find out just what that clue was. More than that, I'd follow it wherever it took me.

He was almost out the door when he turned around.

"I think you may have forgotten to ask me about your pear, chair, and tree. What language would you like me to repeat it in?"

"What?" I asked, uncertain if I'd heard him correctly.

"Choose any language."

"Dutch." A perfect choice, since I knew it and it wasn't widely spoken.

"Een vÿfenzeventig jarige oude man, zes foot lang met een brandende honger. Op een hete dag, wandelde hÿ langs een perenboom en ontdekte een peer buiten zÿn bereik. En zocht naar een manier om die te pakken te krÿgen. Een oude bruine stoel lag dichtbÿ en hÿ ging eropstaan. Bÿting in de vrucht, hÿ genoot van de smaak en van zÿn geluk."

"That was flawless," I said incredulously.

Gabe blew right past that remark.

"I think you have a knack for storytelling, Doc."

Ponderings

In my profession, there's very little time to think between patients. Almost always, appointments are scheduled back to back, and one session can easily overlap into the next person's hour. That's especially true when they're in a crisis.

When someone is spilling their emotional guts, they can't really control the timing and pace of what comes out. On countless occasions a patient would drop an emotional bomb at the very end of the meeting. I had become pretty proficient at tying up heavily laden emotional issues within a couple of minutes.

The immediate mission became one of providing some comforting words and, most importantly, a sense of hope that things would either get better or at least clearer. I had learned to move from a couple's declaration of intention to divorce to hearing about a new patient's terminal cancer within five minutes. These shifts had become easy for me to manage.

Gabe, however, was dropping a series of cluster bombs. I had to find at least some time to digest what had taken place in the session immediately afterward while it was still fresh in my mind.

I came up with a simple strategy after our third meeting together. I would clear my next hour and change the scenery.

There's a small pond that lies within a short walking distance from my office. A bench sits at the edge of the water and, on rare occasions, I sit there and collect my thoughts during a break in my day. No one is ever there.

On my first visit, I sat and looked out over the pond with a vacant stare. Perhaps not too surprisingly, my mind was overwhelmed. My plan to begin to digest what had been said to me was lost in a mental paralysis of sorts. Nothing jelled into anything coherent, and I really didn't try to push it.

A light breeze teased the ripples on the water as a single blue heron circled low over the water in increasingly tighter circles in search of a morning meal. Here and there a turtle would catch its breath before disappearing once again under the water. The absolute genius of it all often amazed me, but on this day I just sat quietly in mental silence.

This changed after Gabe and I had our fourth session. I found myself walking to the park with an energetic stride so as not to waste a single movement. My desire was to get there as soon as possible and begin in earnest to meditate on what was going on. He'd said so many things, and it was quite possible to go in a thousand different directions. I wanted to stay as focused as I could and not squander my time.

So I did what any psychiatrist would do. I sat down,

took a deep breath, and let my unconscious mind get to work. One important psychological fact I'd learned early in my career had proved invaluable. The mystery of creative thought lies in the fact that so many things come to mind without thinking directly about them.

The conscious mind is just what we're aware of at the moment. It's a mere fraction of what's going on beneath the surface. Like a pot of boiling water, where we see the tiny bubbles make it to the surface, thoughts are constantly competing to make it to the level of awareness. The billions of thoughts that don't make it still run most of the show. In that sense, the unconscious mind influences much of life.

Before long, things began percolating. Words like depression, sadness, crisis, faith, religion, anger, and free will formed in my mind like random free associations. Normally, I'd use these thoughts to weave together into a meaningful whole a picture of someone's psyche and help them see something of which they were perhaps wholly unaware. I knew that might not work here.

No doubt, Gabe was brilliant. Quite possibly he were a genius. He had a well-thought-out worldview and could express himself in concise, intellectual terms. Running right along a parallel track was the obvious lack of personal insight that is common to most psychotics. He was sensitive to the suffering of humanity, but somehow his own turmoil was objectified. It was as if he were tuned into the source of everyone's suffering but not that of his own. The only reason he was coming to therapy, he claimed, was because humanity was wearing him down.

I watched another heron dive straight into the water and emerge with a small fish in his mouth. If Gabe and I could bring a conflict to the surface, we might be able to address it. We could pick it up, digest it, and use it to help him heal. In order to do that, we'd have to work as a team. We'd steadily create bedrock—a therapeutic alliance designed to help uncover what he was really suffering from.

Pieces might be coming together, but I still had very little to go on. I knew I'd have to accelerate the pace, because something told me I wouldn't have much time with him.

Session Five

. . . THE JOURNEY WITHIN

"**B**efore we begin talking about me, there's something I want you to know," Gabe said.

"What's that?" I asked.

"I know you might be a little hesitant to ask me certain things. You probably wonder whether or not I have any imperfections or blind spots."

"It's occurred to me," I answered.

"You remember that I said earlier on that I have limitations?"

"Of course," I answered.

"Can you accept that?" he asked.

"It's what I've been waiting for." A follow-up question quickly came to mind. "Why is it important that I understand that you've got limitations?"

"It would be helpful to me," Gabe answered.

"Why?"

"I need to come here and let you see some parts of me that no one ever sees."

"What's it *really* like to be you?" I asked.

"I feel isolated a lot because there's this expectation that I can be leaned on and that I can't possibly have needs of my own. There's this belief that I have no problems and that I'm flawless, and all people have to do is pray and everything will be great for them and for me."

This was another good time for me to be quiet because he was about to let out a landslide of pent-up feelings.

"The idea that God needs to talk to a therapist? Most everybody would find that to be ridiculous except that it's really not. It makes perfect sense. In the time you and I have been sitting here, 15,118 people have been born and 6,304 have died. That's just births and deaths. Many were not peaceful, joyous births and deaths. What about everything going on in between? No one can really fathom that, because it's beyond human comprehension."

He turned his head and seemed to stare right through the dark curtains that hung over the window and out into the world beyond.

"You know, Richard, it's an odd feeling to be connected to everyone and everything and yet experience a disconnection at the same time."

"You feel alone sometimes?" I asked.

He glanced into my eyes for a moment.

"Go ahead and pick any problem you choose. Just make sure it's something that's a human-initiated problem."

Initially, I was confused by the directive but then quickly figured out where he was going with this.

"Atrocity." That word just came out of me.

At that moment, something very strange happened. In one nanosecond Gabe's glance turned into a stare that went right through me. He began a staccato recitation of facts. His tone of speech was flat, completely devoid of any affect, and frankly, unnerving. Gabe suspended his warm, friendly style of relating and replaced it with one that was almost businesslike. It could be accurately described as "matter of fact."

"Here's a tiny fraction of what's going on right now in that particular category," he said.

"In six minutes, a man will be shot in the back of the head in an alley in my name. He won't die right away. It will take four minutes, and he'll cry out for me. In one hour and eleven minutes, a young soldier will lose his life as his truck passes a roadside bomb. His death will be quick. He has no idea because at the moment he's sharing a quick meal with his buddies and cracking jokes. The young man who placed the bomb will die himself in two weeks.

"Right this moment, a seventy-one-year-old grandmother

is screaming for her life as she's being raped. She'll be left to die after being beaten and tortured. A six-year-old child will be introduced to prostitution by her mother. A drug dealer is beating an informant to within an inch of his life. A political prisoner is being tortured, and his cries go unheard."

His tone returned to normal now.

"Those are just a couple of stories. The ripple effects, the suffering of their families, will be enormous. We don't have time to really get into this in detail, but you get the picture, Richard."

"Horrible," I said somewhat weakly.

"It *feels* horrible," he said. "Now take that very narrow example and think of the fact that when something major happens, all at once, I'm completely taxed. A good example of that might be a nuclear weapon. Can you imagine tens of thousands of souls crying out at once? Nothing in the natural order of life has prepared me for that kind of pain. I've been through that one a few times already."

"You believe you witness a lot of suffering," I said.

"You don't really understand."

Gabe paused as he gathered his thoughts.

"I don't just witness it; I'm affected by it. I'm not separate from people."

It was my turn to glance toward the window. What had

begun as a fascinating case of a man with an elaborate psychotic process was now something that began to alarm me. Gabe was seriously disturbed. His ego boundaries were all mixed up. Now was the time to repeat the magic question.

"Do you ever think about hurting yourself or others?" An affirmative answer would open the door for potential inpatient treatment. I immediately decided that if he had any of these thoughts, then I would ask Gabe to voluntarily sign himself in. If not, I'd commit him for his own protection.

"No, Doc. I never do. There's no criteria to commit me."

The last thing I wanted to do was test Gabe's defenses, but the time was at hand. If we were going to move forward, I needed to discover more of what his vulnerabilities might be. A basic rule of thumb was never to pull back a layer of psychological armor without putting something healthier back in its place. Since I was in wholly uncharted water right now, I was definitely about to be flying by the seat of my pants.

"I must say you sounded pretty detached when you were describing the atrocities before," I said.

"That's right. I often have to do that to conserve my strength," he said.

"What's behind that detachment, Gabe?" I asked.

"Self-preservation," he answered as his eyes closed.

"And that helps keep some of the sorrow in check."

"You don't have to take on the burdens of the world, Gabe."

So far, I hadn't seen any of the subtle movements of body that a person reveals as an element of their character. Gabe's motions were reflective of grace and peacefulness. There was virtually no wasted motion or any mannerisms that demonstrated a human quality.

That suddenly changed when I noticed a small drop of moisture begin to form in the corner of one eye. I'd seen that happen tens of thousands of times before and waited patiently as his forehead and facial muscles twitched ever so slightly. If he let himself go, I knew that Gabe's tears would begin as a slow trickle and build into a steady stream down his face. Finally, it might even progress to sobbing. I found myself almost desperate to have this happen.

A single tear moved downward over his cheek. His emotional side was going to come out at last.

"Do you hear that?" he asked me as he opened his eyes and we returned to the present.

I paused and listened for a moment. "No," I said. An immediate sense of frustration came over me as I realized that this chance to see some actual feelings was going to be thwarted. For now.

"It's a siren. You'll hear it soon enough."

We waited for perhaps a half minute or so until I finally heard the distant wail of a siren that screamed by the office, becoming faint again until it disappeared into the silence.

"That's David Levine. He's a forty-two-year-old stockbroker who's just had a massive heart attack while having lunch with a client. It will be touch-and-go for the next few days."

Gabe appeared to be scanning his mind for more data.

"I can't begin to describe all the drama of life going on right around here. Two people will die up the street at the hospice, one from brain cancer and the other from AIDS. An eighteen-year-old boy will celebrate his birthday tonight and drink too much. He'll have a car accident at 1:58 AM within a mile of here.

"This office building isn't exactly quiet either. On the third floor a woman just found out last night that her husband of sixteen years is having an affair with her close friend. A father is worrying over the fact that he hasn't heard from his twenty-year-old daughter in nearly a week. She's serving as a field medic somewhere in a war zone.

"The depression that a man is experiencing is deepening, and he is thinking about taking his own life. A young mother of three will discover in two months that she has breast cancer. The everyday worries and fears that the sixty-three people working in this building are having would keep you busy for your entire career."

That all sounded like a series of random guesses except for one fact. I knew about the father whose daughter was a medic. He was an accountant on the third floor, and I chatted with him occasionally. Gabe probably knew him, too. Quite a coincidence.

The David Levine story was a crazy guess, as was this nonsense about predicting the car accident later that night. I had to admit to myself, though, that he thought fast on his feet.

"You definitely have a lot on your mind, Gabe," is all I said as we ended the session.

Kryptonite

I was completely lost in thought as I sat down on the bench. Luckily, my twelve o'clock appointment had cancelled, so I had two hours to meditate on everything. I thought to myself, *That cancellation was just a coincidence, right?*

I took a deep breath and got to work. The first thing I did was make a cell phone call to the hospital's emergency room. I had admitting privileges there and the staff knew me well, so getting information would be relatively easy.

The triage nurse was on the line in a matter of seconds.

"Yes, Dr. Johnson, the patient is a forty-two-year-old male admitted about a half an hour ago for an acute MI. Do you want to speak with Dr. Garcia?"

"No, that's okay. What's the patient's name?"

"David Levine."

I did my best to not sound stunned.

"What's his condition?"

"Stable. We're going to send him up to CCU in a little while."

"Thanks for your help."

I put the phone down and tried to make sense out of what had just happened. Gabe couldn't possibly have known about David unless he was psychic. Maybe that was the answer. He was extraordinarily sensitive to the feelings of others, and perhaps that was the genesis of his delusional system.

Something else immediately gnawed at me. He told me about my past and David as it was occurring, but could he really predict the future as well? What about that eighteen-year-old boy? If it were true, then why wouldn't Gabe prevent it from happening? I couldn't exactly try and round up every eighteen-year-old in town and ask their parents to keep them in for the night. Besides, he'd said it was an accident. He didn't say how bad it would be.

I decided that the most pressing issue that had come up in our session was self-preservation. What did Gabe exactly mean by that? He had been almost detached when he'd described the suffering people were going through. His tone had changed dramatically from casual conversation to dead seriousness. I sat quietly for quite some time as I pondered this point.

Self-preservation usually meant that conditions warranted measures that were designed to avoid harm or destruction to self. As far as I could tell, since I hadn't seen any evidence that Gabe was an aggressive individual, that meant that his energy might somehow need to be conserved. By extension, that implied that his psychic energy was perhaps a resource capable of being depleted.

Gabe's initial admission that he was tired made absolute sense. He wasn't a machine. He was a feeling, caring, loving person who could feel pain and suffering. But there was something more than that going on. The evidence so far seemed to point in the direction of someone who was not only tired and burdened but perhaps in danger as well.

How could Gabe possibly be in any kind of danger? I thought.

I reviewed some of the things he'd said in earlier sessions. He'd started out by talking about people and shared his role in the world as an architect. From there, Gabe had touched on spiritual matters. More recently, he was beginning to talk more about himself. Without question, that's what I wanted.

An obvious fact then struck me. He hadn't said much about what was good in the world yet, but I was hopeful that Gabe had an optimistic side. We needed to join forces and energize his faith in the positive aspects of life—not really life in general, but specifically his life. Without hope, there would be no desire to get better.

A strong breeze caught my attention as it whipped through the branches of a nearby cypress tree that hung over the pond. One branch in particular waved back and forth gently at first, and with one sudden gust, it snapped and fell into the water, sending a slight ripple across the pond.

Gabe, posing as God, wanted me to believe that he was vulnerable and that his weakness was us. People's actions had the power to strengthen or weaken him. Human beings were the source of great joy and, in Gabe's mind at least, God's kryptonite.

He was a remarkable patient with a vibrant, detailed fantasy life and amazing psychic ability. That much was certain. But more than that, Gabe was an enigma. His mind represented a conundrum to be figured out, and whereas all other patients sat back and let me do the sorting, he insisted on making me part of the puzzle.

A regular guy? My ass.

Second Thoughts

At seven o'clock that evening I retreated to my study at home. It's a tranquil space surrounded by hundreds of books reflecting my favorite authors. The soft beige colors of the walls, combined with a half dozen orchids, help me to decompress after a long and, at times, interminable day of helping people with their personal crises.

I would typically pick up a book, often at random, and read at least a few pages in hopes of finding a temporary escape into another world. I made a point to end my day in this room in search of some measure of serenity. In reality, however, I never could completely get away because, over the years, the pain and suffering of others had managed to permeate every brain cell.

One would think that the constant exposure would have jaded me and that I'd be less affected by it all. Somehow, I should have learned to leave the office and put it all behind me, switching my mind to the off position, or at least to standby. That wasn't how it worked. Something that had happened that day would trigger a series of thoughts and emotions. Almost always, I could find a way to put myself in my patient's shoes.

The more years that I practiced, the more I saw myself reflected in the stories of others. I had passed, or was passing through, many of the life experiences of my patients.

I sometimes believed I was seeing glimpses of what might be up ahead. Witnessing the novels that were their life, I recognized many familiar pages.

But it also went beyond my practice. Nearly everyone I came into contact with became a source of interest. I wondered about their needs and worries. What trials had the cashier at the supermarket experienced in her life? Did the truck driver on the highway passing by me have a wife? Were his parents alive? Where was he born and raised? People's stories, real and imagined, consumed me.

So, at the end of the day, the most I could really hope for was for those cells to keep their noise down for awhile.

Certainly, there would be no peace at all on this night, and I didn't expect any. Pulling the shades closed, I settled into my reading chair. I stared for some time at the orchids. On every other evening, I would marvel at their beauty and the genius behind their creation. For now, all I saw was the contradiction of wonder and tragedy. I saw a world that held such amazing grace and one in which so much unnecessary suffering takes place.

A flood of thoughts entered my mind. At first, I found myself entertaining ideas about the bigger picture of life. Gabe's metaphysical ponderings had touched a nerve.

Like everyone else, I could understand accidents, illness, and natural disasters. That was the part of the natural course of events. It was all the nonsense that troubled me. The intentional pain inflicted on others. The gross immaturity of simply not trying to live in peace with respect for the welfare and beliefs of others. Getting along with each other shouldn't be that difficult. God had given us all the tools and plenty of time to figure out how to use them.

Life was tough enough without making more problems for ourselves. I'm not a politically minded person, but I found myself thinking more about world events than ever. There were dangerous, close-minded ideologies in play that claimed to have the exclusive seal of God's approval on their side.

It was disheartening to think that many of the world's most powerful leaders seemed not to be able or willing to progress beyond a playground conflict mentality. As far as I was concerned, they all needed group therapy.

My thoughts returned to Gabe. I decided that he and I had at least one thing in common. We were both emotionally exhausted. The source of my fatigue lay in the nature of my work. His could be found rooted in his psychosis.

It had to be tiring as hell to actually believe you're God—not just to have the thought, but to be consumed completely by that belief. Gabe was about as separated as a person could be from the rest of humanity. His estrangement was so complete that his only psychological recourse was to invent a persona that still permitted a connection to the real world. That bridge came in the form of the delusion that he was a divine being.

In the private mental world that he inhabited, there existed an internal logic. That system of thinking explained why he felt the pain that he did. His extraordinary sensitivity to others needed an anchor in the real world, and he found it. The central problem was the fact that it was burning him out. The risk that he would fall even deeper into a psychotic state was very real.

I would have to practice some real brinkmanship here. I could neither acknowledge that I believed any part of this psychotic process, nor appear unsympathetic to his story. I had my work cut out for me.

My reflections were coming full circle now as I considered myself. I always did that when thinking about my patients. As a therapist, it was imperative that I stay on top of my own issues to be truly effective. I had a good handle on most everything by now. The only Achilles' heel that still made me vulnerable was my tendency to be disheartened on occasion.

Though I was well aware and appreciative of the blessings in my life, I'd been depressed for several years. Much of my life had been a private strain, and my work had taken its toll. I sincerely believed that I'd helped many people, but at a steep price.

At different times, I would cope by overindulging in

whatever struck my interest. Self-medicating with antidepressants hadn't ultimately worked. They were all short-term fixes that didn't really solve anything. Mostly though, I just felt sad. Nothing could ameliorate the sense of resignation that I sometimes felt when hearing endless stories of human suffering of all kinds.

The paradox of being a therapist who struggles with depression was a challenging way to live. My own personal pains could run deep, but I kept them to myself. I had become an expert in encouraging others to reveal their vulnerabilities while cleverly hiding my own.

Gabe's plight touched my Achilles' heel. I felt sad for him, and it reminded me of myself in some odd way.

The evening turned into night as the day surrendered to the darkness. I stared at the only source of light in the room. The liquid crystal display on the digital clock read 8:28 PM.

I just sat there in the dark for hours with only the silence and the knowledge of what Gabe had said to keep me company. Try as I might, I couldn't dismiss the prediction he'd made about the car accident. My intellect told me it was absurd, but something inside of me just would not let it go. Eventually, I drifted off to sleep.

At 1:55 AM, I abruptly woke up. I wondered in those last three minutes why I hadn't asked Gabe for more details. I should have gotten the street address. Then I could have gone there and witnessed it or maybe even prevented it.

Stop thinking about all this crap, I told myself. You're tired and not thinking clearly. Nothing is going to happen. All you need is a good night's sleep. By the time I'd looked up at the clock again it was 1:59.

I closed my eyes, and felt impatient with myself for being sucked into Gabe's lunacy. I took a sleeping pill and followed it with a strong vodka chaser. I wandered off to bed and looked forward to being unconscious for the next few hours.

I woke up at about six the next morning. I didn't remember falling asleep and certainly didn't know how I ended up back in my study still wearing my clothes from the day before. It took me a few moments to get my bearings, but everything came back to me quickly enough.

I turned on the television and started some coffee. I sat back and sipped with my eyes closed, half listening to the broadcast.

The field reporter's voice came on in the carefully rehearsed way that their voices often do when reporting something they're supposed to feel bad about. The tone had an air of feigned caring that was pretty impressive for this hour of the day.

"Police reported an early morning accident here in the Falls section of the city. The driver, described as a young man in his late teens or early twenties, was killed instantly as he was thrown from his car after hitting a tree at speeds that police estimate were in excess of ninety miles per hour. There were no witnesses to the accident, and authorities suspect it was alcohol related. His name is being withheld pending family notification." The reporter turned to look over his shoulder at the wreck as he added, "Live from the Falls, this is Channel Six news."

I sat up straight and mumbled to myself, *"more like dead from the Falls,"* with some sarcasm. The car resembled a crumpled tin can that was wrapped around a tree that looked as though it hadn't lost a splinter. The glaring white camera lights panned back and forth over the wreck while blue and red emergency lights helped to create a surreal effect. The boy's body could be seen at some distance, covered by an official-looking yellow tarp. Police were taking measurements, and onlookers whispered to each other. The scene was all so dramatic and impotent.

On any other day, it would have been like any other passing news image. I would have forgotten it by the time I poured my next cup of coffee. Like most people, it would have been filed in my brain's temporary storage bin under the heading "Local and global tragedies." In light of world events, that file was constantly full. It was hard for it not to be an abstraction, unless it hit you personally.

"One soldier killed today" doesn't mean much unless he or she happens to be your son or daughter, husband, wife, or friend.

What I found really outrageous is how many things in the world weren't more offensive. Conditions in life that we find collectively intolerable should never have the psychological oxygen to survive. Unfortunately, humans are the consummate adapters, and most everything can result in habituation over time. These were the types of thoughts that went through my mind whenever I watched the news.

Today, things were far different. I would never get that image out of my mind. I turned off the television and thought about his parents. Had they heard the news yet? Probably. No doubt, they were in shock. Eighteen years ago they'd celebrated his birthday, and now he was dead. A child who dies before their parents defies the progression of natural events.

I wished I wouldn't have to wait another week before Gabe and I had our next appointment.

Who's calling me this early? I thought as the phone rang.

"Can I see you this morning, Richard? I'd rather not wait a week," Gabe said.

"How do you know my home number?"

"You've got the eleven o'clock slot open. Is that okay?" he asked, ignoring my question.

"I'll see you then, Gabe," I said in a subdued voice.

"Peter Arnold is at peace, Richard, and his parents will get through this," he said.

"What are you talking about?" I asked with some sudden annoyance.

"We'll talk more about it when I see you."

I hung up the phone, shook my head from side to side, and took a deep breath.

"This is nuts," I said out loud. But it's still got to have a rational explanation, I thought.

Session Six

. . . THE ARCHITECT

The morning commute to my office took me right through the very intersection where Peter had lost his life a few hours before. A couple of burned-out flares marked the spot. Otherwise, there wasn't a sign that anything unusual had taken place. I glanced over to where his body had been and saw nothing but cars passing by in haste, their drivers oblivious to what had happened there.

There were two patients to see before our appointment, and I somehow got through those hours.

Gabe and I took our respective seats, and he began the session.

"Quite a night," he said.

"That's an understatement," I responded.

"Have I been challenging for you?" he asked with a slight hint of playfulness. That question didn't fit the situation, although it came as a sort of unexpected, welcome relief.

"Oh no, Gabe. It's pretty common for someone claiming he is God to come and see me in therapy. Brainless work really. I deal with this kind of thing all the time and could do it in my sleep."

We both laughed for a moment. Seeing that he had some range of affect after all was a very good sign. It was also a welcome respite from all the seriousness. For a brief moment, I entertained a fleeting fantasy that Gabe and I could break out of character. I could stop being the psychiatrist and he the crazy patient. We could sit and converse about philosophical matters and both go on our way refreshed by the discourse. That could and would never happen, of course.

We were locked into our roles, and the presence of his mental illness prevented anything more. The moment Gabe walked into my office, he was the patient. That relationship would never progress beyond therapy. It was that way with every single patient and a reality of my chosen profession.

"Do you trust in me, Richard?" Gabe said in a matter-of-fact way as the tone turned serious again.

In a sense, that was a loaded question. I trusted that he believed in everything he was saying, yet I had to be careful not to validate any of his delusions.

"Yes," I responded. "I believe that you mean well, and that you have faith in everything that you're telling me."

"That's a careful response, but I'll take it. Good news, because I have trust in you as well." He hesitated for a moment as if to let that statement sink into my brain with full effect and then proceeded, "Do you have room in your schedule for another patient?"

"Yes, but I can only handle one of you at a time, Gabe," I said in a nervous attempt to regain some levity.

"That's fine, Richard, because there is only one of me. I'd like you to see Marla Arnold. She's the mother of Peter, the boy who died this morning, and she needs your help and will be calling you very soon."

"How on earth do you know *her*?" I asked.

"I know everyone."

That answer didn't satisfy me. He clearly didn't know everyone, but this forecasting of Peter's death coupled with sending his mother to me for treatment was a real confounding variable that I couldn't readily explain. For the moment, I quickly brushed it off as a coincidence.

"Yes. I'll see her."

"Great. Now, it's time for me to explain something

that's important for you to understand. It's a basic principle about how my nature moves through the world. You remember in the very first session together that I described myself as an architect."

"I do," I said.

"The fact is that I choreograph for good purposes only. I put people together in life only to help each other. I have no role in connecting them for evil purposes. In that sense, people are sent into each others' lives for a reason. While there are both random encounters and intentional crossing of paths, the ones I design work on our behalf. I say our behalf because the work of good is a partnership.

"I can't promote love in the world without the help of people. Without that help, I'm basically powerless. When someone acts with love, caring, compassion, and kindness, they're instantly aligned with me. The key word here is 'acts.' I'm not affected by intention that doesn't translate into some kind of implementation. Actually, Richard, the only difference between what some would call a saint and a regular person is *consistency*.

"Good and evil are self-evident. It may require some work to get past some of the smoke and mirrors, but the clarity of what is right and wrong is there if you look closely enough. They're forces of energy that reside both within people and between them. It's an empirical truth that's based on a simple observation of life.

"Now, here's where free will comes in. People who put their energies together for evil purposes are acting outside of my sphere of influence. My power is enhanced by good, positive energy, and it's depleted through evil, negative energy.

"There is no such thing as too small a contribution. Conversely, there's no negative action, no matter how seemingly insignificant, that doesn't weaken us. Now, wrap your head around this, Richard.

"The welfare of the world doesn't rest on my shoulders; it squarely rests on each and every person who is capable of contributing. It's the absolute inherent responsibility of those who are privileged to be in a position to give, in any way, to share with those who are less fortunate. That's a common denominator that's independent of background and culture."

Gabe paused for a moment as if to consider a thought.

"I realize that this could all sound like just a bunch of pontificating, but there's nothing abstract about Peter dying this morning. His terrible and premature death is very real. His mother's shock and prayers are like an alarm that needs to be answered. There are alarms going off everywhere in the world, some of them noisy and some silent. The question is, what are you going to do when you hear it? Turn away and expect someone else will respond, or immediately understand that you've been made aware of it because you're needed. The alarm could be a simple request from a neighbor across the street. Or it might be a passing ten-second TV image of a group of desperate souls you'll never meet, thousands of miles away, in urgent need of relief from hunger, disease, or war."

"I understand that, Gabe, but what about overload? There's so much need in the world in so many ways that one person can easily be paralyzed into inaction." That sounded weak to me the very second I finished saying it.

"That's a poor excuse. I'm not looking for each person to burn themselves out in an attempt to change the entire world. I am asking that each person work hard to do the right thing within his or her own unique capabilities. Listen, Richard, I'm God, and I can't do it all, so what does that tell you?"

"It tells me that, as your shrink, I still feel like I'm not getting something about you. I don't quite understand the bottom line about how you're affected by everything."

"Okay, Richard, here's the bottom line. I'm suffering," he said.

"I understand that you're suffering, but there's more to it than that," I countered with a slight push.

"Isn't that enough?" he asked.

I knew at this point in our relationship that Gabe did not want to be engaged with just a yes-man. He wasn't interested in someone who would be mesmerized by his presence and in awe of everything he said and did.

Gabe picked me because he knew that at some point down the road I'd gently challenge him. It was an integral part of my profession to do that. No, it was more than that. It was in my blood. He knew that, at some point, I would respectfully suggest that perhaps he was more human than divine. Somewhere imbedded in his unconscious psyche was the knowledge that he wasn't God. He was a fallible human being just like all the rest of us.

Smart, psychic, and very sensitive but utterly human.

"No, Gabe, it's not enough."

I sat still and waited for a few minutes, and neither of us said a word. I wasn't going to break this standoff. I needed to hear what I knew was inside of him. It was there just waiting to come out under the right conditions. I hoped that these were those conditions.

"You think you're a pretty smart guy, don't you, Richard?" Gabe said smiling.

"No, not really, but you're claiming to be the designer, remember? You say you put us together for a reason." I couldn't help smiling back.

"Wise guy."

"So tell me, Gabe, what's behind the suffering and pain?"

"Loneliness," he said. "In most ways, I'm on my own."

I watched for some change in his affect, but there wasn't any. The words were spoken with only a barely perceptible air of resignation–the type of resignation that, say, a parent might have with a child who doesn't listen after being told hundreds of times not to do something.

"Therapy can be a real pain in the ass, can't it, Gabe?" I asked as the session came to an end.

"I'll see you next week, Doc," he said as he left the office slightly faster than usual.

Marla

It would be fair to say that when Marla called me for an appointment I was confounded. Not shocked really, as he'd told me about her, but just surprised that he predicted she'd come in to see me. Gabe must have known her in some way. Maybe she was an acquaintance. In any event, I couldn't easily shake the uneasiness that he had predicted her son's death. There was no question from the news story that it had been an alcohol-related accident, so I could at least rest easy that there had been no foul play involved.

Marla was a small-framed woman with black, shoulder-length hair and chestnut-brown eyes. Her deeply tanned skin stood in sharp contrast to the white sundress she wore at her first appointment. The dark circles around her eyes and swollen cheeks had been touched up with a small amount of cosmetics, applied with minimum effort to look just presentable enough to go out.

A bright gold crucifix hung around her neck, and I quickly learned of her habit of twirling it around with her fingers when she began to get emotional. Marla was a kind woman with a gentle demeanor. Originally from Costa Rica, she explained that she had moved to the United States after meeting her husband, an American who'd been vacationing in her country. Over the years, her mother, two sisters, and a few cousins had managed to immigrate to America. Their family bonds, typical of those from Central America, were strong, and she visited with her relatives frequently.

I knew that she was feeling both an urgency to get to the point of why she was there and yet a dreaded avoidance of it. I imagined that she might be having that surreal experience people sometimes have that if you don't talk about that which you desperately do need to talk about, somehow it won't become real.

She smiled nervously as she told me of Peter's birth, his childhood, and shared milestones that parents are proud of. A few anecdotes bought her some more time, but there was no turning back. It would come quickly now.

Marla was on a one-way track that led to the inevitable

truth that her baby was dead. Her mind was accelerating. The look of shock and horror on her face seemed to arrive at that emotional realization just a fraction of a second before the rest of her caught up with what was going on. She'd gone through this already and would have to go through it many times again.

A whimper suddenly signaled the union of her emotions with her understanding. That only lasted for a brief moment before it was replaced with a gut-wrenching crying that comes from some other world of pain.

Marla cried and cried. Sometimes she would catch just enough air to say his name or apologize for her breakdown.

I knew that at this early stage of grief, the best way I could be of help was to encourage her to let it out. Time and the demands of life would work together to help suppress some of those emotions soon enough, so it was important to encourage a release. In reality, Marla would never be far from that pain. No one who loses someone they dearly love ever completely gets over it.

After some time, she dried her tears and composed herself. She looked to me for guidance, and her eyes held an almost childlike desperation. I wasn't caught off guard. It was that familiar time in the personage of a therapist where reality comes head-to-head with hope.

Fortunately, I've mastered the skill of providing that

hope in the context of reality. My words and my nonverbal messages are chosen very carefully to provide just the right mix of genuine empathy, respect for their pain, and an absolute sense that I will be responsible for their psychological well-being. Each person and circumstance is unique, and so is the instantaneously formulated mix. It's critically important not to mislead and not to set up false expectations.

I helped Marla reconstitute some of her defenses as best I could, and we set another appointment. I recommended that she have her husband come in with her, but she said he rarely shows his emotions, not even now. He'd been distraught for a few days after the accident, but he returned to work and told her flatly never to mention his son's death again. She said that he was acting so normal it was odd.

Marla hugged me tightly before leaving and thanked me. I wished that I could say that I felt something from that embrace, but I really didn't. I was sad for her, but it was more intellectual than emotional. It was the detached acknowledgment of suffering that comes with being battle hardened. No more complex than that.

As we headed for the door of the waiting room, I glanced down at her chart looking for the name of her husband. My intention was to reiterate an invitation that he was welcome to come see me anytime or simply call.

Steve Arnold. I knew that name from somewhere, though I couldn't place it right away. I hesitated at the door for a moment.

"Marla, is your husband from around here?"

"Yes," she answered. "He's lived here his whole life." After a short pause, she added, "except for when his father was transferred to New York for work. They lived there for two years and then moved back here."

Something was coming back to me, although I couldn't place it yet.

"Where did they live in New York, do you know?"

"Long Island. I think the town was called Hunter or something like that."

"Huntington?"

"Yes. Huntington. That's it. He didn't like it there very much."

Oh my God, this gets crazier by the minute, I thought to myself.

"Have Steve call me anytime he wants. I can help you both get through this."

She hugged me again, and this time I felt some emotion. It was very slight, but I did feel something. For me, that was more than a little unusual.

At the end of the day, I switched places and lay down on my couch and stared at the ceiling. I wanted to try and piece some of this together. I had grown up in Huntington myself, and vaguely remembered a boy in my fifth-grade class whose last name was Arnold. That was such a long time ago, and I couldn't be sure. I closed my eyes and remembered back to those days and tried to recall his face.

Then it hit me. I sat straight up and began to pace around the office.

Steve Arnold was the kid my friends and I used to make fun of on the playground. He was a little over-weight, and we teased him relentlessly. It was mean and cruel and immature and what ten-year-old boys do some-times. He'd moved after sixth grade, and we never let up on him. It was one part of my childhood I felt ashamed of.

What were the chances that he and I would be living in the same town now and that his wife would seek help from me, of all people, after his son dies a tragic death?

It was probably another coincidence, but not one that I could easily explain away.

That evening, I drove through the intersection where Peter had died and noticed what appeared to be a memorial set up by the side of the road. I pulled over and studied the tribute. There, placed in the dirt, was a large white cross surrounded by plastic flowers. A few cards, some in Spanish, were wrapped in clear plastic, sealed shut and taped to the cross. A framed and enlarged high school graduation picture of Peter dominated the scene. It was the same as the wallet-sized edition Marla had proudly shown me earlier. His wide smile and handsome face full of promise didn't belong on this cold road. It belonged with the living.

I studied it carefully and noticed his eyes. They were an unmistakable deep blue and reminded me of something long ago forgotten. They were his father's eyes.

The Cavalry

On very rare occasions, I've consulted with another therapist over an especially challenging case. Ethically, such a practice was permitted so long as the situation truly warranted an outside perspective and any identifying information was kept confidential. I was well aware of the fact that I'd promised Gabe that I wouldn't violate his request for privacy, and as such, I struggled with my decision for quite some time.

This case was way too complex and important for me to stand by and not get another opinion. In the end, I decided to take some action.

I gave a lot of consideration to who might be the best choice. On my first pass, I realized that someone locally wouldn't be such a great idea. My reputation was important to me, and the last thing I needed was for the word to get out that I was struggling with a psychotic whom I believed was psychic. That wouldn't fly.

What I really needed was someone outside of my professional sphere whom I trusted. After careful deliberation, I realized that the best person to call would be a former professor of mine, Dr. Harriet Reynolds. She held both an M.D. and a Ph.D. in religious studies and was well known as a recognized expert in the interface of psychiatry and mysticism. The perfect combination. Definitely the person I was looking for.

A Web search indicated that she'd written over one hundred journal articles on the subject of psychiatry and various spiritual matters. More important, I remembered her as a thoughtful, open-minded woman who might be able to give me a fresh insight into Gabe.

I contacted the department of psychiatry at Yale and was pleased to learn that she was a professor emeritus who still taught an occasional seminar. I left a message asking that she please call me at her earliest convenience. I wasn't expecting to hear from her that very evening. Her gentle voice and the calm tone in her speech exuded a sense of welcomed sanity.

We caught up with some generalities, and I told her the reason for my call. After graciously agreeing to hear the case, I reviewed everything in detail. She listened intently and asked a few questions for clarification.

"So what's your impression, Dr. Reynolds?"

I think I was expecting some immediate explanation for all of this. There was a moment of silence, and I imagined her sitting in some dark, wood-paneled study carefully digesting my words. I hoped her mind would search over the many years and thousands of cases and provide me with a coherent explanation for all of this.

My real wish was that she'd tell me that, though rarely encountered, Gabe's psychosis was an established disorder, found cross-culturally perhaps. As I would soon find out, it wasn't going to be that clear cut.

"A fascinating case and highly unusual. He has some classical delusional material but coupled with exceptional intelligence and purported psychic sensibilities."

"They're not purported, Professor. There's no question he has some kind of gift."

"The elements independently can be found in various conditions, but taken together don't support any known disorder. I've never come across this in any culture."

There was a long pause.

"How do you feel about Gabe?" she asked.

"Like you, I think he's fascinating."

"No, Richard, I think he's intriguing because I've never met him. You might find him mesmerizing. It's you who is sitting across from him, and apparently he's reading your mind and that makes it entirely different. How do you feel about him?"

"I like him."

"Why?"

"I can identify with a lot of what he's saying. Aside from the fact that he's psychotic, there's value in what he's saying."

"So basically, his thoughts and views mirror your own . . . exactly?" There was something in Professor Reynolds's tone that shifted slightly, as if she were honing in on something.

"Yes."

"And what's your impression of how Gabe feels about you?"

"That's an interesting question. He's engaging in a strange sort of way and yet detached from me personally. I feel as though I'm someone who simply meets his requirements."

"And what does he seek to accomplish by seeing you?"

"It started out as a claim that he wanted to vent, but it's evolving into something else. I feel like there's some momentum building up, but as to where it's headed, I don't know."

"I have some advice for you, Richard. For now, continue what you've been doing. He wants to tell you his story, and it sounds like he has quite a tale. We both know he's psychotic, but maybe you should treat that as incidental . . . for now at least. When spiritual matters co-vary with psychiatry in this way, we're better off suspending judgment until we've spent more time with the patient."

"You don't think I should confront him head-on?'

"It won't matter at this point." She cleared her throat and then added something.

"Be careful with this case, and keep me informed as to what happens, will you please?"

"I will, but be careful in what way?"

"He's got some very special abilities, you can be sure of that. I know you don't need reminding, but don't get distracted by his intellect or spiritual acumen. He's still a man in pain."

Session Seven

. . . PONDERINGS

I entered the waiting room and had Gabe's coffee in my hand as I extended it to him.

"Do you mind if we have today's session over by the pond?" he asked as he accepted the cup.

That was a tough request. It was an unorthodox practice to see patients outside of the office. More importantly, I controlled my environment, and out in the open, I could be perceived as being more vulnerable. On the other hand, Gabe might be more exposed himself.

Before I had a chance to object he said, "Good, I'll meet you over there," and he turned to leave.

I walked out right behind him but he was already gone. I looked up ahead, as my pace accelerated to nearly a jog, but there was no sign of him. When the bench came into view, I saw him sitting there already, cup in hand, looking out over the water. Not a hint of being out of breath.

I reasoned that it was a very clever parlor trick of some sort. He had planned it in advance and no doubt wanted to use it as supporting evidence of his claim to be God, yet there was an unmistakable queasiness in the pit of my stomach that argued otherwise.

"That ought to be physically impossible," I said as I sat down beside him trying to catch my breath.

"It's spiritually possible. In reality, I don't have much control over the physical universe. I can't stop that bird from diving into the water and picking up that particular fish." He pointed off to the sky and at just that second, a heron took aim, plucked a small fish from the pond and flew away.

The sensation in my gut went away as I reconstituted my conviction that while Gabe had many intriguing aspects to his makeup, he was still hopelessly delusional. He had to rationalize his inability to influence the physical world somehow. It would be both interesting and revealing to see just how he would do that.

"No control?" I asked. "Wouldn't God have complete influence whenever he wanted to?"

"Very limited and used on special occasions only. I

would never let some of the crazy things that people do go on if I could actually stop it."

Gabe was going to sidestep the issue of his lack of power because facing it head-on would permit the contradiction of his own view of himself as God and his human limitations to materialize. Psychotics don't care to deal with the inherent absurdity of their beliefs. He returned his gaze to the water. I had the feeling that I was in for a lesson.

"Why do people come to see a therapist, Richard?" he asked.

"Many different reasons," I answered.

"Right, but the core reason is they're dealing with some kind of chaos in their lives, some element of disorder. You asked me in the beginning what brought me some peace, and I said that one of the things is nature."

"I remember that."

"This ordinary pond is a stunning example of the beauty and perfection of nature. You know that because you've spent many hours here, but you've missed something important every single time. Do you know what that is?" Gabe asked as he turned his complete attention to me.

"You're forever thinking, Richard. It's your blessing in life and your curse. You've never just lost yourself in life because you're too busy analyzing it. You also worry about everything and everybody too much."

That was the truth. Under different circumstances, I could take that observation and run with it as I had many times before. It was tempting to ask Gabe why he thought I was like that, but the inescapable fact was that this was his therapy, not mine.

"Why did you refer Marla to me?" I asked.

"So you could help each other. Marla was also sent to help you."

I didn't buy that and thought that if my brain had eyes of its own, they'd be rolling around right about now. If he was really so in tune with me, then he'd know how burned out I can get and depressed. How would having yet another distraught person come into my life help me out?

"Follow me closely on this, all right, Richard?"

"Okay," I said with a little bit of impatience.

"You're so caught up in your psychological reaction to life that you're missing the fact that each act of goodness in life is an opportunity to make you spiritually stronger. You have trouble connecting your actions to your spiritual well-being, but they go hand in hand.

"Feeling better in your life when you help someone out would be a nice by-product of your efforts, but it's unnecessary. You have a job to do. Period. *Everyone* who is capable has a job to do. This life isn't a time to slack off. Trust me: there will be plenty of time to rest later. There's more. Are you with me?"

I nodded an affirmation.

"In our last session, you suggested I might be mad. I don't ever get angry, Richard. Most people in the world believe I can be punitive. That would be completely antithetical to my makeup. Punishment is one of the poorest learning tools. My power rests with the good in people, which brings me to my next point.

"If the truth of a statement could be assigned a weight, I'd want what I say next to be worth a trillion pounds. *There is enormous good taking place in the world at all times*. That goodness is found in the people who practice it, and it's going on everywhere, and it doesn't need any explanation."

"I understand that," I said.

"Good," he answered. Gabe took a final sip of his coffee and turned his body toward me. "Marla was a special gift."

"I'm not sure I understand," I responded.

"You've figured the connection out on your own already. But let's take it from the top. When you were a child, you and her husband Steven attended the same school. He was in your fifth-grade class. You used to make fun of him and call him names. He hit you once, and you gave him a black eye. Steven cried, and you and your friends laughed at him." Gabe spoke with his usual complete conviction that what he was saying was simply a matter of record.

"How does helping Marla fit into this?" I asked.

"She fits in perfectly. This is your opportunity to do something kind in return for something you've done in the past that was hurtful. Steven loves Marla but can't give her the support she needs right now. Helping Marla also helps Steven."

"You're telling me this is some sort of karmic payback?"

"No. I'm telling you I gave you this gift of being able to help someone you've hurt. That happens on rare occasions, but one would have to be a fool not to take advantage of it."

This was out of my comfort zone. Too New Agey for a conservatively trained shrink.

"It was nice of you to invite Steven to call you, but he won't."

"And would that be because he'll figure out I'm a bully from his childhood?" I asked.

"No. He doesn't hold any grudges. Steven is not the kind of person who reaches out for help."

Gabe paused for a moment.

"Let's move past this," Gabe said in almost a dismissive tone. "I have an assignment for you, Richard."

"Not so fast," I said. "How do you know all these things?"

"I'm God."

I could tell he wasn't going to budge. If only he would consider the fact that he wasn't God, maybe we could get somewhere. It wasn't time to confront him. There was still value in delving deeper into his psychosis. Professor Reynolds was right on point.

Gabe probably never had anyone listen this long to this fantastic story. If this was his day in psychiatric court, he was entitled to speak his mind.

"All right," I said. "What's the assignment?"

"Before we get together for our appointment next Tuesday, I want you to visit Pittsfield."

"Why Pittsfield?" I asked.

"That's where your grandfather is buried," Gabe said.

When he said that I had to consider the possibility that Gabe was taking our relationship too far. I had to entertain the thought that he was gathering information about my personal life that had nothing to do with any kind of psychic ability. Perhaps he was becoming a stalker. I couldn't rule that out. If he was stalking me, had he gone to Pittsfield himself and researched my background? Did he know where I lived? Had he been there? I'd been stalked a couple of times in my career, and it was a very unsettling experience.

Asking him directly would yield no satisfactory answer.

He would just say that he was God and that would be it. There wasn't enough evidence to warrant an abrupt end to therapy. I immediately decided, though, that if any of my privacy was breached, psychotic or not, I would stop treatment immediately and refer him elsewhere. As these ideas went through my mind, I knew that once again I was seeking a logical explanation for Gabe's incredible ability to know things about me.

In the end, crazy as he was, the suggestion to travel to Pittsfield wasn't. If I decided to go, I would not tell him, of course, because agreeing to go would only reinforce his belief that he had some control over me. That would be antitherapeutic.

"That's a nice suggestion, Gabe. Maybe someday I will get there."

He responded with a smile that seemed to say that he'd humor me by tacitly accepting my answer.

Pittsfield

The drive to Pittsfield took the better part of a day. It was a pleasant journey on a country road through rolling hills and farm country. I was grateful to finally have some time to think about everything that had happened so far, without distractions.

This guy by the name of Gabe shows up in my office one day and claims he's God. I conclude that he's a paranoid schizophrenic but adjust my diagnosis to atypical psychosis in light of his unique delusional constructs and absence of other symptoms. I decide that my best course of action is to be neutral about his claim as I want him to trust me. I will neither acknowledge nor refute his assertion.

Gabe wants to come and see me for sessions because he has this need to vent. The pressure of dealing with people's problems takes a huge toll on him. He explains that he is a limited resource and needs his energy to be continually renewed through the goodness of people's actions.

Gabe's not partial to religion but says it's fine if people use it as a blueprint to act with kindness. He's a little cagey on the subject of what he can or can't control in the physical world. He tells me that he's basically a spiritual choreographer who puts people together for good reasons only. Then Gabe predicts a death and asks me to help soothe a grieving parent's pain.

Now I find myself on this trip to visit the grave of my grandfather, a man I idolized as a child.

Okay, Richard, those are just the broad strokes. What's really going on? He claims that he is just coming to you in the form of a patient because he has to. But why does everything you've seen and heard fit closely into what you conceive of God as being? He's open-minded and not very judgmental. He's burning out, limited in power, and an exhaustible resource. So far, there's nothing in his nature that you don't lean towards agreeing with. In fact, he appears to share many of the same philosophical views that you do.

So is that the deal? You can only see in him what's already in you yourself? Is Gabe some kind of reflective mirror? Sure, in part, just like every patient is to some degree. But that's way too simple.

Gabriel says that he's not looking for adoration or submission. He claims to want a partnership. That much is clear. It's not the naturally occurring stresses of human life that are getting to him, it's all the self-generated nonsense.

He's extraordinarily aware of people around him and clearly a gifted psychic with an apparent ability to predict future events. That in itself is amazing. Yet he has a huge blind spot. Gabe is completely oblivious to the fact that his own issues emanate from within himself. He believes that his distress originates from the problems of the world. Gabe labors under the oppressive delusion that he is God and that everyone else's problems are his own.

The psychological defense mechanism of projection is serving to protect him from the deep psychic pain associated with his mental illness. It's a solid defense that won't be abandoned easily.

The sun was beginning to set behind a mountain ridge as I entered the town and searched for a hotel. I hadn't been here in over twenty years. On at least a hundred occasions, I'd told myself to just get in the car and go pay my respects to my grandparent's memory. It seems, though, I concluded, that everyone has a Pittsfield in their lives.

The hotel had a back porch with a sweeping view of the mountains. I made it there just in time to catch the last light of the day. The shades of greens were magnificent and provided me with a reminder of God's amazing creativity. There was no doubt that whatever else there might be in the world, there was natural beauty as well.

I tried to get to sleep at a reasonable hour but found that I was too restless and more than a little curious. I had planned to get up in the morning and head straight over to the cemetery. Instead, I began a slow, meandering trip through a fragment of my childhood as I drove the streets in search of my grandparents' home.

I had their address and a rough idea as to where they had lived. For some odd reason, I didn't want to ask for directions.

I spent quite some time looking for a marker that might jog my memory. Finally, something in the corner of my eye caught my attention. It didn't take long to recognize the playground across from the church we had attended when visiting town. I was getting warmer. Since memory is associative, I knew that details would start coming back. Wasn't the church across the street from their house? It didn't take long to find it.

The playground looked remarkably intact after all these years, although it seemed much smaller than I remembered it. The carousel, slide, and swings sported a fresh coat of paint. I parked my car and walked around for a few minutes and thought about how strange life was. In another time and place, I had been there as a child visiting my grandparents. Memories began to flood my brain as I thought about my grandmother.

Oma, as we called her, was a strong, spirited Russian with a heart of gold. She could give you a bear hug that would take the wind out of a sumo wrestler. Her cooking consisted of hearty potato and meat combinations that I've never remotely seen again in my life. The aromas were rich and inviting.

I remembered how she would call me, my brother, and each of my sisters into her bedroom one at a time before we finished our visit. She would have each of us kneel on the floor in front of her as she made a sign of the cross and blessed us. As a child, I thought of it as a stupid, necessary chore. As an adult, I could now look back on it as the act of love it was.

My grandfather held a special place in my heart. Opa was the kindest man I ever knew, next to my own father.

I never saw him angry, raise his voice, or behave in any way other than selfless and patient. I was happy to see him every time and sat mesmerized by the stories he told as we fished together. I was under the spell that a child has for someone who is bigger than life.

The years passed, and with them the family road trips back to see Oma and Opa. Obligatory calls on holidays and birthdays were all that remained in the last years of their lives. The passage of time widened the gap between the joys of my childhood and the distractions and responsibilities of being an adult. One of my regrets is that I didn't put in more of an effort to stay in touch.

Growing older, I understood that my grandfather couldn't be perfect. He had to have flaws that I never knew about. My professional training and experience convinced me that everyone had issues. All you had to do was pay close attention, dig a little, and you'd find some unresolved conflict or dynamic, yet my memories of him are untarnished and I was grateful for that.

Their house was still there but looked old and tired. It had the appearance of a structure that had endured countless seasons and weathered many storms. The red brick façade was peeling in many places, and the landscaping was overgrown. Not unlike the playground, it seemed much smaller than my memories predicted it would be.

I saw a For Sale sign in one of the windows and

wondered who, if anyone, might be living there. Lost in my own world of thoughts, I didn't hear the man approach from across the street.

"Hi, can I help you?" he said in a guarded tone.

"I was just passing by, and I remember this house, that's all. My grandparents used to live there," I said, trying not to look uneasy.

"I'm Tom Harris. I own that house now. Glad to meet you." He extended his hand to shake mine with the kind of genuine friendliness that one finds in this part of the country.

"Nice to meet you, Tom. I'm Richard Johnson," I said.

"You're Anthony and Marina's grandson," he said.

"Yes. You knew them?" I asked.

"Sure. I bought the house from your uncle after they both passed, but I knew them from church. Kind people, your grandparents."

"Thank you," I responded. It felt good to have this connection with my past.

"You want to come in and have a look around? The inside looks better than the outside," Tom said.

"Are you sure?" I asked.

"No bother," he said as he took the lead and began walking toward the front door. "No one else lives here anymore. It's just me and my dog. He's friendly enough, once he gets used to you."

Passing through the front door was like passing through a time portal. Instead of that sense of discomfort one often feels when entering someone else's home for the first time, I felt relaxed. Safe.

"Take your time, I'm going to go out back and check on the dog."

He went out the back door before I could register a polite protest.

I instantly remembered the layout and moved slowly through the house, savoring each room. Tom was right. The inside was in better shape. Seeing the home filled with the furniture and personal belongings that reflected another family's life was a strange experience. My intellect told me that this was now someone else's home, but my emotions couldn't put that in any reasonable context.

The child inside of me registered a protest. These things don't belong here. Oma and Opa belong here . . . and I belong here, in a perpetual childhood, where stories are spun, delicious home-cooked food is served, and there is an abundance of love and laughter. Where no one ventures out and learns about a hard world.

I didn't feel any conflict as I walked from room to room, ducking my head into the doorways. It had more of a sense that a person has when they become aware of what one gained and what they lost along the way, hitting you at the same time.

Just as I almost felt an urge to cry, I heard Tom call out from the kitchen, "Hey, you want a beer?"

"You've been very kind, Tom." I almost followed that with a refusal and insistence that I'd already overstepped my welcome and needed to leave. Instead, I thought that he might be lonely and wanted me to stay a little while.

"Sure. Thanks," I said as I sat down. "I'll have one and get out of your hair."

"No need."

"Why are you selling the house?" I asked.

"My wife died of cancer about two months ago. It was a long fight. Too many memories in this house," he said.

"I'm sorry."

"That's all right. We had a good life together. I'm thankful for what we had. No need to wallow in the pain. I've got a cabin that's been in my family for years. It's about forty miles from here up in the mountains."

"So that's where you're going?" I asked.

"Yeah. Like I said, there are too many reminders here. I thought I could adjust, but her spirit's in this house. Do you know what I mean?"

"I do," I said.

"So how was your trip down memory lane?"

"It was good to be able to come inside. Thank you."

"It's been some time since we were small enough to slide down that slide, don't you think, Richard?" Tom said as he pointed toward the park. We were both around the same age, I guessed.

"Quite some time. Seems like another lifetime ago," I said.

Tom's eyes squinted slightly and from that emerged a frown. He seemed to be searching through his memories. It was as if he were looking for something that had been hidden away for a long time. A smile signaled the fact that he'd found it. A nodding of his head added emphasis to what he was about to say. I could tell before the first word came out that he'd recognized me. But how?

"Remember that kid who fell off the top of that slide and they took him to the hospital? Do you think he died?" He said with a smile and a laugh.

"Pardon?"

This was weird. I remembered the event completely.

"How could you possibly know about that?" I asked with surprise.

"We used to play together sometimes when you came visiting your grandparents. You don't remember, but I do."

"You're kidding."

"No, and luckily, I didn't die from that fall, but I did end up with one hell of a concussion, I can tell you that."

I found that astonishing and made no attempt to hide the expression from my face.

"Why are you so shocked?" Tom asked.

"What are the chances of this?"

"The chances of what?"

"You just happen to live in my grandparents' old home. I run into you and you invite me in to have a look around. Then I find out we played together as kids and we catch up over a couple of beers like we're old buddies?"

"I think it's cool," Tom said.

"It is cool, but you've got to admit that it's strange," I said.

"Why's it strange?" he asked.

"Things like this don't just happen every day," I said.

"They do in my life," Tom said as he got up to stretch his legs. "Just got to open your mind to things. Do you believe in God?"

"Absolutely."

"Then just accept that he's putting us together all the time. I don't overanalyze this stuff. Just accept it as a gift. You're too analytical, Richard."

"I get paid to be that way. It's my career."

"What kind of work do you do?" he asked.

"I'm a psychiatrist."

"A shrink? That figures."

We talked for a few hours about all kinds of things. The time went by with the kind of pleasantness that friends have when they reconnect after a long interlude. I learned that Tom had been through a great deal in his life. Both of his parents had died when he was an adolescent, one from cancer and the other committed suicide. He'd been a combat medic in Vietnam and had been seriously wounded in the back. One of his two daughters had been born developmentally disabled. Had I not heard thousands of tragic life stories like Tom's, I might not have believed it.

In light of all he'd been through, one would expect that he might be a bitter man. Tom was just the opposite. I felt humbled by his optimism and positive attitude toward life. He would often say that other people had a far worse life than he did. He managed to find gratitude, and I admired him for it.

Finally, I got up to leave and knew we'd never see each other again. I thought that he knew it as well.

"You're more than welcome to come up to the cabin, though you might not like it. You don't seem to be the outdoorsy type."

"That's a fact," I said as I shook his hand good-bye. "Thank you for a great night."

"It was fun," he said.

I was getting into my car, and he leaned into the window.

"Hey, you know, we didn't talk a lot about your work. I'll bet you've got some interesting stories to tell."

"There are a few."

As I drove off into the darkness, I wondered what Tom would think if he knew I had a patient who was claiming to be God.

The Cemetery

The Pittsfield Cemetery lies near the center of town. It was a beautiful day, and the air was crisp with the freshness of mountain air.

I parked the car and began my search. I knew that my grandparents had been buried together and that their headstone was of a simple marble design with a cross at the top. That much my mother had told me, though she couldn't recall the exact location.

Walking up and down the rows of headstones, I found myself thinking about the stories behind each one. I wondered about the lives that they had lived. They had no doubt laughed, cried, loved, hated, and perhaps gone through drama that seemed so important at the time. Silence now dominated this sacred place.

Some of the ground had been freshly dug, while in other places centuries had gone by.

An interesting row of headstones caught my attention. One was etched with an ornate ivory cross. Next to it was another equally crafted headstone that bore the Star of David. The third one in line was of some special interest. I couldn't see the headstone right away, as it faced in the opposite direction.

Peering around I saw immediately that it was the crescent and star that symbolized a Muslim body turned to face Mecca. Finally, at the end of the row, stood a simple marker devoid of any religious symbolism with the inscription "John Simmons rests here." Could he have been an atheist?

This unusual mix seemed somewhat contrived, especially for a conservative town like this. What were the chances that a Christian, a Jew, a Muslim and an atheist would be buried together? No sooner did that thought cross my mind when I saw a marker in the shape of a pyramid at the head of the row. An inscription there read, "It doesn't matter what a man believes . . . what matters is what he does with that belief."

Certainly there were open minds everywhere, even places where you least expected it.

At last, I found the headstone and was pleased to see that it stood in a place that received ample sunlight in the mornings and late afternoons. It was of a simple design, and the cross at the top stood firmly on the headstone as if it was a permanent sentinel keeping watch over their souls. A fine, hairline crack in the granite ran from top to bottom, but otherwise it was in good condition.

It was a strange experience to see their names together along with the dates of their births and deaths. A brief, one-line engraving read, "May God watch over their souls." Clearing away some twigs and leaves that had gathered at the bottom, I placed the bouquet of flowers I'd picked up that morning.

Even though my adult life had been spent appearing to be the model of psychological health, it was very difficult for me to actually get in touch with my own feelings. My patients, family, and friends came to me for help and advice, and I was expected to have all the answers. Here, in the presence of Oma and Opa, I could be myself. No one would see me, and I wouldn't have to be strong or in charge. I wanted to honor their memories, but I also sought a catharsis. A watershed . . .

A small concrete bench, perhaps the size of a loveseat, stood about ten feet or so from their grave. I took a seat and let my mind travel. I found myself remembering things about my grandparents that I hadn't recalled in years: the way Oma smelled like a fresh bar of soap, Opa's calloused hands that reflected a life of hard work in the fields, Oma's dancing with Opa when they heard a favorite song on the radio. They were images of childhood and innocence and a simpler time, impressions that seemed an entire lifetime ago.

Whatever ability I might have had to attach that feeling to any event or thought was suspended for the time being. For now, in this moment in time and space, I would not have to interpret anything to anyone . . . not even myself. I could experience whatever came up in a raw, unadulterated form—a mess that wouldn't have to be cleaned up.

With that realization, I began to well up some tears. Sadness immediately mixed with a sense of satisfaction, as I hadn't cried in many years.

The crying turned into gut-wrenching sobbing as I became consumed with grief. My body shook with a release of tension that to an observer would have looked like an exorcism. It was as if my body finally had its opportunity to express itself after tens of thousands of hours of calm, unmoving control in the face of the unfathomable suffering of others.

This sobbing went on for quite some time. I remember my first rational thought as I came out of it. I recall telling myself that I wanted it to go on. This was my chance to get it all out before I would seal it up again and put on my game face. But my rational self kicked back in. I pulled it together, and just as suddenly as it began, it ended.

Walking away, I turned back one last time to say good-bye, knowing I'd never return.

Looking in the rearview mirror as I drove, I saw Pittsfield recede into the background as I headed home.

The decision to pick up my cell phone wasn't the result of anything that I thought of. It was pure impulse.

"Thank you again for your kindness. Do you think a city boy could find something to do in the mountains some weekend?" I asked.

"That depends," Tom answered. "Can you get by without the Internet and cable television?"

"I'll do my best if that invite is still on the table."

"It is. But remember: if you come visit me, there are two rules."

"And they are?"

"You can only have fun, and you're not allowed to think about work."

"That's a deal."

I felt really good for once, and I savored the feeling of being happy for the moment.

Session Eight

. . . WISH LIST

Marla came to see me again, and it went fairly well under the circumstances. She had built up some strength, and with that some hope. For my part, I looked at her presence in my life a little differently than I would have prior to meeting Gabe. In fact, I was seeing all of my patients in a different light. My work was still hard, but now it seemed a little less burdensome. "How was your trip?" Gabe asked as he handed me a coffee that he brought in with him. I quickly ran my gaze over the plain white cup, looking for a product identifier.

"You don't really think I got this from Starbucks or Dunkin' Donuts, do you?" he asked me with a grin.

"That would be one hell of an endorsement, Gabe," I responded.

"So?" he asked again.

"It was a good trip," I said. "Thank you for encouraging it." I wasn't really all that shocked that he knew about it.

"There's a reason I suggested you go there, Richard."

"And what's that?" I asked.

"You had to see and feel something firsthand that I couldn't just tell you about. Remember at the very beginning of therapy I told you that I wasn't going to be looking at your life in detail? That I wanted to be off duty in here?"

"Yes, I do."

"Good. I want you to tell me what you felt in Pittsfield." He hesitated a second before adding, "Did you visit your grandparents' home?"

This last question threw me off track. He had convincingly demonstrated his psychic prowess with me from the very beginning of therapy. I reasoned that if he simply had elected to, then Gabe could quite possibly know everything he wanted to about the visit. He would know about Tom and the gravesite and every single thought and feeling that I'd had.

The good news was that he hadn't followed me. That supported the encouraging notion that Gabe wasn't stalking me. At the same time, something was stirring from deep within me. Gabe's question triggered a conditioned response that I almost invariably had with all patients at some point. Even though it didn't exactly apply in this situation, it came up nevertheless.

It didn't take long to identify the tiny current of doubt that began to tug at my conscious mind. If given attention, that current could quickly build into a stream that would be hard to deny. The stream would gain its inevitable momentum and turn into a river with a separate path of flow that I surely couldn't ignore. With any other patient, I'd track it separately and consider its utility later.

With Gabe, I would have to come forward. I'd have to admit that I had come up against the familiar two-edged sword found in my work: the time when both the moment of truth and doubt come alive at the same time and struggle for dominance and, finally, survival.

Every patient has a story to tell, but it's much more than that. They also have one to sell. The need for acceptance and understanding is primary, and when anyone is telling me their story, they are also asking me to buy it.

It's like watching a magic trick for the thousandth time. You know that much of it's illusory, but it still pulls you in. There's a part of you that wants to be tricked. That's until something happens to change it up. It could be very subtle, like a body movement that doesn't match what's being said, or easily identifiable like an obvious contradiction.

It's not as if they're lying or even trying to exaggerate. It's more like their version of reality is their truth, and how could it be otherwise? Many times, another person comes in with a completely different view of the same event, and you would swear that they lived in two separate and distinct worlds. In the end, the genesis of doubt is as varied as people are themselves.

So when Gabe asked me about my trip, an automatic, ingrained mental current immediately formed and turned around and around in increasingly tighter circles until it formed a sentence that spoke silently in my mind.

Do you doubt him? Of course you do. He's engaging and insightful and there are a lot of strange components to this case, but he's still psychotic. Don't ever lose sight of that fact, Richard. He's asking you about your trip because he has limitations. On one hand he demonstrates amazing psychic gifts but, right here, right now it looks like he's unable to pick anything up. Gabe's assertion that he wants to be off duty is a smokescreen to cover the fact that his talents are limited.

"A little late in the game to wonder who I really am, don't you think, Richard?" he asked. "It's all right. You're making the same mistake everyone does when it comes to me. You want me to act like God all the time. Very well then. You searched for their house and found it at 8:33 PM. At 8:36, the owner Tom Harris comes up behind you unexpectedly and asks if he can help you. He thought you might be casing his house, but your own friendly, non-threatening response calmed him down quickly. As I'm sure you might have guessed, I choreographed that meeting, Richard. I wanted you both to cross paths."

Once again, this was nothing short of astounding. He pegged everything perfectly.

"You believe you choreographed that?" I asked in an almost desperate search for something to say.

"Let's get back on track. I don't want to read your mind. I want to hear your words. What did you feel when you were there?"

I took a few deep breaths and regained my focus. That was my own magic trick. He was asking me how *I* felt. I had to be careful here because the therapy was never supposed to be about me. Still, these were highly unusual conditions to work under. On very rare occasions, I might share a personal experience with a patient if I judged it to be potentially helpful. But a small disclosure could lead to a line of discourse where the focus shifted in favor of the shrink's own problems. That was never acceptable.

Gabe was no ordinary patient. His extraordinary sensitivity warranted some self-disclosure on my part.

"When I went through their house, I felt sadness over what was lost," I said.

"And what did you lose, Richard?"

"The same thing everyone does. I lost my childhood and with that my innocence." There was one more thing to add to the list. "And I lost my dreams."

"Lost, or modified by reality?"

"Both."

"And what was the most important wish you had?"

"I dreamed that the people I loved would never die."

Temporarily disarmed, I found myself talking about my feelings and experiences more than I had planned to. I was now violating the simplest and most cardinal rule of being a therapist by talking about my own issues. The emotional impact of visiting my past coupled with Gabe's pointed questions temporarily breached a kink in my professional armor. I would regain it immediately, and with it, control of the therapy.

"I had to give up some dreams, too," Gabe said.

That surprised me, though it probably shouldn't have.

"What do you mean?"

"Do you think an architect doesn't have a vision in mind when putting something together?"

"You had dreams?" I asked.

"I did. That's one of the reasons I sent you back to Pittsfield. I wanted you to feel that loss . . . to really know what I was talking about."

Admittedly, I can be a bit slow on the uptake, but the picture was starting to come together.

"What was *your* dream?"

Whatever casual friendliness he'd ever shown me in the past was on hold now. He answered this question in the most serious way imaginable. Gabe's body didn't flinch a millimeter, and his concentration on what he was saying was absolute. It was as if this was *his* chance. This was an opportunity to tell *his* story.

"I always envisioned that people would get along in peace. They would cooperate with each other and never intentionally hurt each other. They would use their combined gift of intelligence and free will to create a life where they would appreciate each other, and honor the earth which, not too surprisingly, can look a lot like people's conception of heaven.

"Now, just so you don't think this sounds too much like an idyllic greeting card, realize that I experience the real world. Pain and suffering are a part of natural life. I never dreamed of a conflict-free world where everyone holds hands and sings songs. But conflict between people can either be managed with love, compassion, and tolerance, or it can regress to ridiculous levels. I never imagined a world where so much intelligence can exist alongside such stupidity. Genius in the pursuit of something inherently foolish isn't genius at all. In my view, any fool can build a more effective weapon, but a really creative individual, or nation, finds a way to improve the lives of others.

"I'll be here in perpetuity. Long after everyone is gone, I've still got the same responsibilities. I'm here making an appeal, Richard. I'm sure you figured that out some time ago. I need both individual and collective help. Plenty of people are on board, but there's a lot of crazy people left out there who believe they're right, and let me tell you, a lot of people suffer over what's 'right.'

"Let's get back to my dreams. I couldn't have a childhood in a human sense. I had an original plan, so just think of that as my childhood. Time and experience revealed that my hopes weren't going to be realized. That's resulted in me adjusting my expectations in light of reality. Many people like to think of me as a teacher, so let's use that idea for the moment.

"I expected, and put all the tools in place, for the entire class to get an A. Right now, I'll settle for a C, but that's another conversation. The interesting part of all this is that a great many individuals are doing just fine. They are earning a solid A in this life. The issue is the bigger picture. We're all responsible for each other, and the only way the whole class can move forward a grade is if *everyone* passes.

"A part of you is probably thinking, what difference does all this make anyway? The answer is that the purpose of life is to enjoy it as best you can and believe in whatever you want. There's only one caveat. Respect and take care of each other. Enjoy your spiritual free will. I don't care about how you choose to view me. There's even room for those who don't believe in me at all. A person won't burn in hell if they don't follow a certain path, but neither do they have a fast-pass ticket if they blow each other up in my name.

"Tolerance isn't a lack of spiritual discipline; it's an essential component of it. Confidence in your own beliefs includes the willingness to accept the fact that others don't see the world in the same way. That's it. End of story."

Gabe's demeanor returned to normal. He took another sip of coffee and waited for me to respond. I didn't know what to say.

"I know it must seem like I'm detached sometimes when we talk, but you of all people should know why that is."

"I have a pretty good idea," I responded. "But why don't you tell me anyway?"

"Because otherwise I'd implode."

That hung in the air.

"Any more questions?" he asked.

"Do you believe that your forward movement, graduating to the next level, depends on what everyone else is doing?"

"Not the way you might think of it. When someone carries some of the burden, no matter how small that contribution might seem to them, it makes more of that resource available somewhere else. The positive energy can flow to where it's needed most. It's a dynamic system that follows natural laws and seeks to fill any void created by its absence. The vacuum in this case is the empty space where I don't exist. In a sense, it's almost scientific, don't you think?"

"So, you're saying that God is still evolving. God is incomplete and imperfect?"

The way I put that question was purposeful. If Gabe would consider talking about God in the third person, then we might be finally able to put some distance between him and his mental creation.

"Since I am God, Richard, and the source of everything, I'm telling you that yes, I am still evolving myself, though I don't have imperfections in the way people normally have them. My thinking also has to change to mirror an evolving world."

That's outrageous and should be painfully clear to Gabe, I thought to myself. The idea that God is anything short of complete flies directly in the face of any human notion of God. Once again, Gabe is talking about his own shortcomings as a mere mortal.

"You have a very interesting mind, Gabe," I said. He was indeed an insightful and brilliant man. If I could just free him from his illness, then possibly we could find a way together to channel that intelligence in a way to help him and quite possibly fulfill his desire to help others. "Very interesting for a regular guy."

"Interesting or not, we have work to do. And only two more sessions to do it in."

"This is going to take much longer than that," I said. "We're just getting started, and we have a lot of issues to deal with."

"You mean curing me of my psychosis? Ridding me of these delusions that you believe that I have?"

Here was my opening. I could choose one of two paths. Either I minimized that comment and continued to play along, or I could seize the opportunity to gently but directly confront his psychosis. With the notification that he would be terminating treatment soon, I decided I didn't have the luxury to wait for a better time.

"Gabe, the belief that you are, in fact, God is a delusion. It's part of a disorder you have, but it's treatable. I'm not questioning your sincerity in your conviction, just the objective truth of it. Plenty of patients end up thinking they're God. You definitely have some very special abilities and a well-thought-out philosophy of life, but in the end, it's reflective of a mental illness."

He sat there just staring at me with a blank look on his face. I needed to continue with my evaluation and follow it up with recommendations.

"I think you've been in some real psychological pain for some time. You're suffering because you have a special sensitivity, some psychic ability, toward others that I simply don't quite understand. That pain is too hard for you to deal with, so you project it outward. Sincerely believing you're God is a way to distance yourself from the pain that originates somewhere inside of you. You and I haven't been able to get close to the source of that pain because I don't know anything about you, Gabe.

"I've learned a great deal about your view of humanity and your take on God's role in the world, but you won't let me into the slightest details of your life. Your intake form lists no address or contact information. No information on family or place of birth or anything that would help me understand you better. It's hard for me to do my work to help you when I have so little to work with."

His stare was unwavering.

"Since I have only two more sessions to treat you, I need to discuss our treatment options. I'd be remiss if we didn't consider medications. There are new classes of drugs that can be very effective in these kinds of cases. They could relieve you of the upsetting thoughts you're having and help reduce some of the anxiety as well. That could be supplemented with an antidepressant, which could elevate your mood. If we put you on medications, though, you'd have to follow up with me at least once a month so we can monitor your progress. The ideal would be a combination of both medications and psychotherapy. This is a lot to digest all at once, Gabe, and I want to be straight with you."

He waited for a long time before responding. I looked closely for some sign of how he was taking this. Was there going to be relief that I was taking charge of something he really knew down deep inside, or frustration that I wasn't buying into his craziness? His face was expressionless.

"Fortunately, Doc, my welfare doesn't depend on your faith or lack thereof that what I'm saying is true. As far as I'm concerned, it's just a detail."

I couldn't help the sigh that came out of me. Gabe was the toughest nut I ever had to crack in my career.

"I know this is frustrating for you, Richard, and I'm sorry."

"I'm trying to help you, Gabe."

"And I'm trying to help you as well."

"How?"

"There was another reason I had you go to Pittsfield." Gabe had that focused tone in his voice.

"And why was that?"

"You needed that emotional release at your grandparents' graveside. Something deeply personal and meaningful had to provide the trigger. There is so much locked up inside of you. Remember, Richard, that above anyone else, I know you through and through. I know your deepest secrets—strengths, weaknesses, and everything in between.

"There's not enough joy in your life. In the time that's left, you need to find ways to be less mindful and more mindless. Learn to enjoy your life in a deeper way.

"The trip to Pittsfield was meant to put you in touch with a simpler time in your life. The experiences that you had as a child aren't completely beyond your reach as an adult. I know you think that having Tom buy your grandparents' home and you running into him that night were nothing more than a coincidence. That's a shame. You're missing the choreography of it all.

"Many of the people in your life have crossed your path for a reason. Tom was one of them. He has a clear role in your life and you in his. The two of you could be great friends. Taking advantage of that, or not, is your call.

I've given you the pieces. Now it's up to you to put them together."

"I have to admit, Gabe, you give me a lot to think about."

"By the way, you made the right decision calling Tom on the way out of town. You're going to have fun together."

"I thought you told me when we began that you'd be off duty in here," I said.

"I changed my mind a little. It's God's prerogative, you know," he said with a grin.

Reflections

That evening, I retreated to my study to take stock of the day. I pulled back the blinds and opened a window. Reaching into a drawer, I pulled out a Churchill-sized cigar. I wasn't a real smoker, but once a month I permitted myself this indulgence, and tonight was the night.

I think it was a remnant of behavior from my college days. Fellow students and I would while away the hours smoking French cigarettes, pipes, and cigars and thinking we had all the answers. We would have esoteric discussions about matters that we thought were so very important while we secretly snubbed the rest of society for being so out of touch with the pressing philosophical issues at hand. What did we know?

As is my custom, I mentally prepared to review the stories of the day, one by one. I felt that it was my duty to spend some time thinking about my patients when I had the time to properly consider them.

In the beginning of my career, I'd spent a lot of mental energy digesting sessions and then planning various strategies of interventions. I had my books and training to draw from. I regularly relied on the intelligence of famous theorists and experts in the ways of human thought and nature. Their eloquent writings and deeply considered treatises on the psychology of people were touchstones that helped guide me in my work.

I didn't simply rely on psychology and psychiatry either. My reference library consisted of books on religion and philosophy as well.

Over the years, I became increasingly aware of the truism that most everyone comes to terms with sooner or later, provided they're paying close attention: I discovered how little about life I really knew. The models of human psychology would always be limited by the very object of their study. The variation in people and their own life stories was so broadband that the smartest approach often became one of controlling assumptions.

I would discover over the many tens of thousands of

hours doing my work that there were very few linear answers because the questions themselves were anything but linear. The questions were based on amalgams of history, experience, and beliefs that were as unique as the individual.

My focus, therefore, became much more tactical than strategic. I stopped trying to make huge changes in people's lives. Instead, the object became one of helping people get through their life crisis by giving them unconditional support and a few tools to take back out on the playing field. I rarely consulted a journal article or book and virtually never planned an intervention, not because I thought I had the answers all the time.

It was much more based on an understanding that the playing field of therapy was very dynamic and changed moment to moment. I discovered that it was in the best interest of the patient for me to adjust my tactical response to actual field conditions. More importantly, people know when you're being genuine or fake. It turns out that trying to force the proverbial square peg into the round hole didn't work well in the psychological world either.

These were the kinds of thoughts that I considered these days. I reflected on my patients' problems more in the context of their whole lives. How did their trials fit into the bigger picture of their lives? Where were they going on their journey, and what part did I have really?

As the years went on, I once again became more philo-sophical. It was as if I was coming full circle.

I took a deep puff on the cigar and watched the smoke slowly climb into the air. Beginning my mental review of the day, I decided quite naturally that I would save Gabe for last.

Angela, my first appointment, was a new patient. She couldn't get into my office fast enough and began crying from the moment she took her seat. It turns out that she had recently broken up with Eric. The fact that they were both married to other people and having an affair was a complication. She had hoped it would be more than just a fling and had gone ballistic when she found out Eric took his wife on vacation. After all, wasn't he supposed to take her to Paris? The root of her affair was a deep lone-liness in her marriage. She hungered for intimacy, and that was compounded by a loss of her father two months earlier.

It was only when Angela began to describe her boy-friend that I realized that Eric and his wife had recently been patients of mine. They had seen me together in marital therapy, and this trip was planned some time ago in an effort to try and put their marriage back together. These ironic crossing of paths happened now and again in my work.

If the truth be told, what I see and hear in a typical

week would keep a reality television audience entertained for months.

Maureen came in next. A response to the letter I'd sent on her behalf had arrived in this morning's mail. I wasn't sure where my attempt at communication had landed on the continuum between rejection and reconciliation. Never did I expect a note from the landlord who indicated that he was so sorry to inform me that the previous tenant, Maureen's daughter, was deceased.

She had died three months earlier, and he thought it not his place to discuss the details and suggested I contact the county coroner's office. He was kind enough to include the telephone number and reiterated that he was sorry to be bearing that news.

I thought about calling Maureen before our appointment and telling her on the phone as soon as I read the letter, but quickly dismissed that option as cowardly and unfair. She needed to be told in person.

When she came in, I told her about the letter and the news it contained. As is often the case in these types of matters, she simply nodded as if she understood and thanked me for trying. The shock would set in later. That would be followed by the guilt and self-recrimination. There would be lots of pieces to pick up when her world would come to a shattering halt.

It was Paul's appointment next. He filled the entire

session with a tirade of disdain for the "system" that was keeping him oppressed and in dire financial straits. A bank was ready to repossess his car for being six months behind in payments. It was their fault for charging too much interest and adding compounding late fees.

Doctors were idiots for failing to cooperate with his worker's compensation claims, and he was going to sue his last landlord for not giving him back his security deposit after he was evicted. The excuse that he'd left the apartment in poor condition with a foul odor was ridiculous according to Paul. The landlord had agreed to pets, and it wasn't Paul's problem that he didn't specify how many. Twenty-seven birds, three cats, and two dogs in a one-bedroom apartment were his business.

Marty came in today. He was in pretty good spirits. His lover had decided that he could deal with the HIV after all. They had a long heart-to-heart talk and would give their relationship an opportunity to grow. The rest of the session focused on what would be Marty's best strategy for telling his mother that he was infected. She had long ago known he was gay and accepted that fact with love and understanding.

With that foundation, I reassured him that although she would be predictably upset, she would be there for him and would handle it. I wasn't saying that speculatively. I knew Marty's mother, as she'd been a patient of mine herself some ten years before.

I was pleasantly surprised by Elaine's declaration that she'd not used anything to self-medicate over the past week since our last session. She'd followed my treatment plan and attended daily recovery meetings and found a sponsor whom she felt was a good fit. Elaine had some cravings now and again, but got through them pretty well. She had an aura of self-confidence that she was going to beat her addictions and begin a new life. Clean and sober would be her new mantra.

Elaine's somewhat cavalier attitude from last week had been replaced by a conviction that she now knew she couldn't ever touch anything again. I supported her actions but tempered it with cautionary notes that she not get too overzealous and the fact that we had a lot more work ahead of us.

Brian was late for his appointment. He apologized but explained that he was caught up in traffic on the interstate. Cars stood bumper to bumper for miles because of an accident. He was completely relaxed. That was welcome news, considering his driving phobia. Brian was thoroughly amazed at the ability of hypnosis to work so effectively. We did another deep induction, and I sent him on his way.

Louis and I had a good meeting. As always, he went over the events of the week quickly so that he could get to something he was really eager to talk about. I could tell that this story was going to be different for some reason.

He had a more serious tone in his voice, and he appeared to be anxious.

Today's story had to do with an ex-marine he'd met at the Veterans Administration clinic. He was waiting for the doctor in the waiting room and struck up a conversation with a guy sitting next to him. Turns out he was a World War II vet also who had served in the same unit as Louis. They made some small talk and, at first, avoided the topic of combat and its aftermath. As is typical of vets from any war, there is often a desire not to talk about what they've seen or experienced.

They began talking about a sergeant who had a colorful reputation in the unit. They laughed a little when recalling his antics until the subject of his death at the hand of a sniper came up. Though that one event, out of so many traumas they'd witnessed, happened over sixty years ago, to them it seemed like a moment ago. Tears welled up in their eyes, and they quickly regrouped.

I found it humbling to hear this story and felt gratitude for Louis and the sacrifices he and many others had made and were still making.

I searched for a common denominator in today's sessions and found it rather quickly. The unifying thread was me. I felt just a little bit better about my work. I began to understand more fully their roles in my life. That was surprising to me as I thought I was past the point of no return in my career.

Gabe's comment about helping others as being a privileged opportunity at spiritual growth wasn't just written off as the ramblings of a crazy person. I was more aware of it, and instead of being so burdened, I experienced something of a small but hopeful sense of satisfaction in the importance of my work. That wasn't a feeling I'd had at all in some time.

Viewing it in this way, today's lineup looked a little different. Angela could teach me about the importance of trust and fidelity. My long-standing relationship with Maureen gave me an opportunity to be charitable. Paul's unremitting complaints reminded me of the dangers of pessimism. Still, his presence also gave me a chance to discover a way to find unconditional acceptance in someone with whom I could not even slightly identify.

Marty's plight was an example of courage, while Elaine represented enthusiasm for fresh beginnings. Brian's gratitude helped me feel a clear sense of effectiveness.

I had nothing but admiration for Louis. He was helping to solidify my faith in the value of commitment and genuine compassion. Perhaps it wasn't all that strange that he reminded me of my grandfather.

I concluded that today's sessions could deplete me further, or I could try to find a way in which they made me stronger. Maybe that was up to me.

Turns out that Pittsfield might have turned out to be

more than just a field trip. Gabe was still psychotic, but he had some valuable observations to share.

It was time to consider Gabe's case.

Now, more than anytime in my career, I would need to read between the lines. There was a far deeper story here. Gabe was such a fascinating case, but I couldn't get a real handle on him. The things he said weren't disorganized or psychotic in their content. In fact, I found the content to be rational. It was the form that presented a problem. This insistence that he was God was the central defining feature of his psychosis. It was deeply and firmly ingrained. Since the magnitude of a psychological defense is typically proportional to the insecurity being protected by it, Gabe was extremely fragile underneath.

Gabe desperately needed some kind of an explanation for what he was experiencing. He somehow had a special ability to empathize with others in a psychic capacity. While I'd witnessed such abilities before, he was in a league that I couldn't readily understand. And that magic trick of beating me to the pond still baffled me.

He found that explanation in the belief that he was God.

It was much more than that. He was convinced that his story contained a message and a purpose that went well beyond himself. Gabe outlined some of his philosophies, demonstrated some interesting abilities, and admitted his limitations. He'd even told me that if he let himself feel everything going on, he'd implode. Talk about the Big Bang theory in reverse.

What stuck me most in our last session was his explication of his dreams through his God persona. While grandiose, those dreams had been tempered by reality. Gabe claimed that the plan hadn't unfolded in quite the way he'd envisioned. There didn't seem to be any bitterness or disappointment attached to that, but rather a cool acceptance. I surmised that Gabe wanted to be perceived as a combination of an idealist and a realist.

The cigar was almost finished, and I was getting tired. Clasping my hands behind my head, I closed my eyes as I leaned back in the chair. It had been a long day.

Drifting off into that zone of being neither awake nor asleep, a thought entered my mind. It came from somewhere between the lines. I remembered that there was a place in everyone's life rooted firmly in the middle of their dreams and reality. It's the place that moves them forward. It's the place where hope and faith have a life of their own.

Gabe has hope, I decided. Convoluted and crazy in its expression perhaps, but hope nonetheless. He wants things to get better, and he wants to believe that they can. In that way certainly, he was just like all the rest of us.

At best, I'd given him some cause to reflect on the possibility that he had an illness. At worst, he would be a psychotic drifting through life. Another lost soul. It wasn't as if the welfare of the world or God's well-being, as I know it, depended on Gabe's improvement.

Two more sessions, and he's gone, I said to myself as I finally fell asleep.

Session Nine

. . . BEYOND THE GENOME

"**B**y now, I'm sure you've guessed that I'm not here just to vent," Gabe said.

"I figured as much," I answered.

"We have one more major point to cover. Then you'll understand the whole back story and why I really came to see you."

The segue from patient to his desire to be viewed as a teacher had been subtle at first. By now, it was entirely clear that he wanted to teach and I to learn. That was an attempt at role reversal. My guess was that everything Gabe had said and done was measured and designed with a certain goal in mind. I would have to be patient a little bit longer.

"This debate that's going on right now over whether I'm real or not is interesting. Fortunately, my existence doesn't depend on belief alone, though it helps if it's used in the right way. The fact is that it isn't really possible to prove or disprove me. That's because I'm an empirical truth—something that's experienced individually, not collectively. Belief can actually be counterintuitive. Belief can exist in spite of the facts. Faith doesn't necessarily follow logical principles. Nothing new there.

"When you were in Pittsfield last week, and Tom asked you if you believed in God, you answered without hesitation, 'Absolutely.' Your conviction is based on your own experience of me. No one else's. That's the way it is and always will be."

I tried not to look startled, but I was. I could feel my body begin to shake as that familiar sensation began in my gut. My whole being was reacting to something . . . but what? Here we go again. How could he possibly know what Tom and I had talked about in such detail? I'd never heard of any psychic being that specific. For the first time, I was having real difficulty finding a place within my own mind to categorize what I'd just heard. I struggled to keep my body movements or reactions from giving me away.

"Faith and science are only at odds if they're pitted that way. There's room for both. Neither party needs to really convince the other, though it is interesting to me that I've never experienced anyone converting to science on their deathbed or screaming out Charles Darwin's name in a time of crisis.

"I like genome research. It's wonderful and magical in a way. It's going to continue to reveal a lot of architectural mysteries in the physical realm as well as the psychological. It will provide a compelling explanation for evolutionary processes. A proclivity toward goodness will be found, but never the mechanism for its actual execution. That's because individual free will and moral conscience will never be fully explained by phosphates and nucleotides.

"What I'm really interested in, Richard, is the development of good that's deliberate and automatic. I want human beings to take the principles of kindness, which are well understood and universal, and make them entirely *unconscious*. Over time, the dream, the hope, is for people to evolve to a point of individual and collective goodness. Teaching and setting an example. Can't get away from those basic learning tools. I'm not going to waste any time going over what to teach. That information is apparent a million times over.

"I have a huge vested interest in all of this. I'm a limited resource, and I need help in either conserving what I have or increasing the base supply. Remember that I know what's coming down the road. Some think that those dynamic forces don't exist and that we live in an indifferent universe.

"Whatever a person chooses to believe, it's time I let you in on a fact. It's a fact that is very often full of misunderstanding and misinterpretation. The universe seeks to balance itself and evolve into its highest most attainable structure. That includes spiritual as well as physical evolution. That which doesn't ultimately adapt will be left behind as an artifact of growth and change.

"There will be accountability for a person's actions. Not a punishing, angry judgment, but an accounting nonetheless. There will be forgiveness and compassion along with justice. That's the consequence and privilege of living as a moral being.

"It all becomes crystal clear at the time of death when a person returns to the collective. The neurons will stop firing, the body will die, and what one thought and believed won't matter anymore. What will matter is what they did with that belief. Did their actions move humankind forward or not?

"Everything in the material world changes form, and theories come and go. Every age thinks it is on the cutting edge of understanding how it all works.

"A word to the wise: Arrogance, whether it's rooted in science or religion, leads to a certain condition of myopia. Narrow vision leads to constricted thinking. Nothing does last forever. Everything evolves and changes. Any questions?"

"Just one," I said. "When you said everything evolves and changes, does that include you?"

"More than anything else," he answered.

Gabe then hesitated for a moment. It was as if he were deciding to add something.

"It should be abundantly clear that my own survival is at stake here, too, Richard."

When he said that, I immediately realized that if Gabe didn't learn to distance himself from the world's problems, he was really going to lose his mind. The world was clearly not going to go through any radical changes, not in any of our lifetimes.

Perhaps he was alluding to the idea that he might not be able to sustain his delusion of being God any longer. If that were to happen, his psyche would collapse in on itself, which would be catastrophic.

Session Ten

. . . THE MISSION

The fact that our course of therapy was coming to an end wasn't unexpected. Right from the beginning, he'd let me know that it would be time limited. Gabe had set down some ground rules, and rather than struggle for control and dominance, I elected to have him dictate the pace and number of sessions. Certainly, as events unfolded and he began to reveal the true depth of his mental illness, I became increasingly concerned for him. More than anything else, I wanted to help him.

I pointedly began to strategize about how I might convince him to continue with therapy. There were options to explore together. We hadn't even tried a course of medications. I would be firmer with him and take charge. I would practically insist that he remain in treatment. On some psychological level, he probably wanted me to implore that he stay in therapy.

The most I could do was try, though if I were a betting man, I really didn't think he'd continue. I could only hope that our meetings were of some value to him. They had certainly helped to change my life.

Patients often teach me something about myself. There is usually some aspect of their problems that I can relate to or at least learn from. Gabe's case didn't really lead me to a personal revelation or anything that dramatic.

The changes I felt as a result of seeing him were more subtle, and therefore more likely to last over the course of the rest of my life. I had to open my mind to the fact that there were some features of his psyche that defied easy interpretation. I thought that I'd truly seen it all over the course of my career. My experience with Gabe changed all that. He certainly wasn't God, but he was gifted in some very profound ways. A heartbreaking case of a genius trapped in a mental illness.

He did say something that shifted some of my attitude toward my work. Gabe had made the point that those who are able to, have a responsibility to help those who are less fortunate. It was both a privilege and an opportunity for self-growth. It wasn't like I hadn't thought about that many times; it was just that the part that he added made great sense to me. He reminded me that a sense of joy is a welcome byproduct of giving, but not a necessary condition for it to take place.

The sadness in my work came, in part, from a sense of too much responsibility for my patient's welfare and neglecting important parts of my own life. The trip back to Pittsfield helped me understand that.

Our meeting approached, and I had a feeling of excited anticipation.

We settled in for the last time and shared a final cup of coffee.

"So, this is our last session," I said as an affirmation.

"Yes, it is."

"I really think you should reconsider, Gabe. There are a lot of things to discuss, and stopping now would be premature."

He paused for a moment as if to give what he was going to say next the proper dramatic effect.

"I've given this a lot of thought, Richard. Tell as much or as little about our sessions as you want."

For quite a while now, I had secretly hoped that this might be coming. At once I felt exhilarated and anxious.

"What do you mean?" I asked.

"Tell whomever you want in any way you wish."

"Who's going to really believe the outrageous claim

that God actually went to see a shrink?" I asked.

Gabe sat deeper into the couch and smiled in his friendly way that had become quite familiar to me.

"Whether it gets received as a work of fact or fiction won't matter. Let the reader decide. Tell the story anyway."

"If that were even a possibility, how would you want me to tell it?" I asked.

"Truthfully. The way you experienced it. I've tasked you with this mission in part because you're mostly nonjudgmental. You won't throw that much of a spin on it. I have faith that there won't be many distortions. I also know that you'll need to present me as a delusional patient."

"Why me, Gabe? You know we can't finish this without my asking."

"You've got the skill set I'm looking for. You're a shrink, and you write. You're not too intellectual, and you understand your limitations."

"If I were to write this book you're talking about, is there anything else you would want me to know or write about?"

"There are a number of people who are on board with the work that needs to be done in the world. People of influence, wealth, and fame. They're part of the change. They serve as role models and teachers. But they're only the high-profile ones.

"There's an enormous amount of good going on quietly

and without fanfare. Everywhere and all the time. Personal sacrifices are made in selfless acts of love all around us. All someone has to do is pay attention, and it's evident.

"Make sure you let people know that I'm an optimist, Richard. I see the good in people. I've based that belief on what I know to be true. Emphasize the need to accept differences and especially the openness to embrace other cultures."

He waited for a second before continuing.

"I know I look pretty average to you, but if you want to see other aspects of my being at any time, just look around you. I really am everywhere. It's not hard to figure out."

I had nothing to say. Somehow, I knew that all of this had come to an end, and the need for questions was over.

"It's been an interesting ten sessions, Richard," Gabe said as he stood up to leave. "Thank you for your help."

"If you ever change your mind about coming back in, Gabe, just call me."

With that, he walked out the door, and I returned to the silence of my office.

I sat there for some time in quiet reflection and wonder. I ended up thanking Gabe for what he'd brought to my life, wishing him well, and pretending he would hear me.

Debriefing

I always conduct a careful mental audit after termination to evaluate my effectiveness and whether or not I could have handled things differently. The quality of the therapeutic relationship is the core element of therapy. The unique dynamic interplay of doctor and patient, if managed successfully, can lead to profound changes under the right conditions.

Termination of therapy can be at the discretion of the patient or the therapist. Sometimes it's based on a mutual agreement that the goals have been achieved. At other times, stopping can be premature.

In Gabe's case, I thought I did reasonably well considering the unique challenges of his delusional system. I had been shaken out of my conceptual comfort zone, though I never breached my responsibility to appear professional and objective.

At the same time, he should never have stopped treatment. He needed help, much more help. If I could have had my way, I'd have seen him twice a week for as long as it took. We'd taper down the sessions as a function of his improvement. A turning point would have been his own acceptance that he was suffering from a mental illness.

He would need to buy into the idea that he wasn't well, though not necessarily in an explicit manner. Insight was not a prerequisite for improvement in psychotics. Many patients followed a treatment plan without admitting that there was anything really wrong with them. In my career, I'd seen many severely disturbed patients take their medications religiously while contending that there wasn't a need for it.

The good news was that Gabe was basically harmless. He wasn't a risk to himself or others. If I believed that he really was, I would have involuntarily committed him long before. Since he refused to tell me anything about his personal life, I had no idea where he lived or how he supported himself. He was well nourished and always neatly groomed and dressed, so I surmised that he had a decent place to live.

As long as he kept his crazy belief to himself, he'd probably pass through life unnoticed by others as an unremarkable individual. If he did talk about his far-fetched ideas, then most people would quickly dismiss them as the rambling of a psychotic. Had he not claimed to be God, then his benign philosophies of life would have provided for interesting conversation.

In the end, I had to accept the fact that the answers to those questions, and many more, would be unknown to me.

That evening I spoke with Professor Reynolds and I brought her up to speed with what had taken place during our last sessions.

"It's unfortunate he stopped therapy prematurely. He is unquestionably an extraordinary man." There was a short pause before she continued. "But I don't agree with part of your assessment, Richard."

"Which part?" I asked.

"His defenses may not hold under the weight of his delusional system. When he refers to his very survival, I think he might be more fragile than you think."

"Suicidal?" My heart began to pick up its pace.

"No. I don't think so." Her tone was reassuring. "It's more likely he'll decompensate."

Clinically, decompensation meant that Gabe's mental world would become increasingly disorganized. His thoughts and feelings would make less and less sense to those around him. Practically speaking, his deterioration would inevitably result in his having a difficult time coping.

A vision flashed through my mind. A mental image of Gabe formed where he was walking the streets aimlessly, muttering to himself and scoffed at by others. He would join the legions of social outcasts. Another mentally ill person with no real home or normal life. It wasn't a pretty picture.

"Whatever happens, he terminated and that's the

extent of it. How do you feel about him finishing?" she asked.

"Disappointed."

"That sounds about right, Richard. I'd be disappointed, too. I have to tell you something. I've done my homework on this case and have never heard of a patient like this in my entire fifty years of practice and teaching. Clearly, he's not God, but if Gabe is everything you've described to me, he's a pretty convincing mortal impostor."

I felt relieved in hearing that. Professor Reynolds was respecting the credibility of my description of Gabe. She never even suggested that I might be distorting things, or even worse, having a problem keeping a grip on reality myself. She'd been a good choice.

"Thank you for your help, Professor . . . and not thinking I was nuts."

"You know what I can conclude after studying and observing and listening for all these years?"

"What's that?"

"We're all a little nuts."

Full Circle

After a week passed, I couldn't get Gabe out of my mind. There were many other patients to consider, but he dominated my attention. I thought about him constantly, and Professor Reynolds's concern for his welfare didn't escape me.

Gabe had most definitely gotten into my head. Frequently, I woke up in the middle of the night wondering where he might be and how he was doing. In the sometimes uneasy and contrived relationship that therapy represents, I had to admit that I missed him. But it was more than that.

I was preoccupied with the unsettling feeling that I was his only hope for a normal life. He wasn't the type of patient who would go to another therapist. For whatever reason, he'd chosen me, and I couldn't shake the conclusion that I let him go too easily. Perhaps I could have been even more insistent that he remain in treatment. I might have suggested periodic follow-up sessions or asked him to at least call me once in awhile.

Another possibility presented itself. Maybe he simply wanted me to contact him. Perhaps he wanted to come back in but was too embarrassed to make another appointment. He wouldn't be the first patient to feel that way.

I decided I would take a chance and try to get in touch with him. That would be a long shot, considering the fact that the only information I had on him was the two calls he had made from a public phone. It would probably ring off the hook or some stranger would answer. I could feel my heart begin to race as my fingers punched in the numbers. The phone rang twice, and for a fraction of a second, I thought the woman's voice at the other end was real until I recognized the recording.

"We're sorry, you have reached a number that has been disconnected or is no longer in service. If you feel you have reached this recording in error, please check the number and try your call again." I rechecked and tried the number two more times until I was satisfied that it was a dead end. It seemed a little puzzling but not completely out of the ordinary. The phone company probably disconnected it since he last used it.

Curiosity got the better of me, and I called the phone company. They gave me the address, and I waited until the end of the day to drive over. I had expected a public phone for communal use in some low-rent apartment area or a convenience store. Instead, the directions led me to a quiet roadside rest area on the outskirts of town, a lightly traveled road that used to lead to a now-defunct resort.

The parking area was deserted. I got out of the car just as the sun was setting over some gently rolling hills in the distance. Down below, in a wide valley, a river snaked its way through the countryside bordered by a few farms. A single hawk circled overhead. It was very quiet and peaceful.

I scanned to each side and, at first, didn't see any sign of a phone. I began to walk toward the other end of the parking lot and finally spotted a phone booth. As I drew closer, I saw that a couple of window panels were missing and one was cracked. It was beaten and weathered. Looking inside, I expected to see the usual graffiti and wear and tear one would associate with a public phone. I wasn't disappointed. But there was something missing. Something that should have been there.

The phone had no cord and no receiver and was covered with what had to be months of grime and dust.

That feeling in my gut came back, and I was on the edge of nausea. I raced back to my car, took a deep breath, and called back the phone company on my cell phone. There was a simple explanation for all of this. Someone had recently vandalized the phone. Plenty of working phones were covered in dirt.

"Let's see," the customer service rep said. "That phone has had a work order ticket on it for the past six months."

"So it's been having problems?" I asked.

"No, sir. It's been out of service," she continued. "There's a notation here that it's not going to be repaired because it's scheduled for removal. We do that when demand falls in a low-priority area. We'll get to it. Sorry, I'm sure it's an eyesore."

"Forgive me. Are you saying it's been completely out of service for the past six months?"

"Completely, sir."

"So there's no way a call could have originated from that number?"

"Impossible."

I sat down on the retaining wall and looked out at the view. I drew a deep breath and considered everything that had happened. It didn't take long for me to conclude that there was too much here for me to rationalize away. My psychiatric bag of tricks was empty. I'd exhausted my supply of logic under the weight of another kind of evidence.

I had to concede that Gabe's claim that he was God was true.

I didn't resist it. I just accepted it. I pulled something

from deep inside myself that I hadn't relied on enough for some time. Faith once again found a place in my life. God had entered my life in this strange way and had tasked me with a mission. It was as simple and complex as that.

At the very instant that I surrendered to this belief, my cell phone rang. It only rang once, and there wasn't any time to answer it. I checked the caller ID and slowly, one by one, four letters revealed themselves. Since I never put Gabe's number in my directory, I accepted it as the sign it was: it turns out I really was God's shrink.

Epilogue

R eaders are free to choose some earthly explanation for all of this. In my view, God came to see me as a patient. It wasn't his charisma that ultimately won me over, it was his humanness.

In accepting this mission, I could now communicate some of God's wishes.

God wants to be viewed as open-minded and didn't exclude anyone from his architectural plan. He favored no single religion and accepted those who freely chose not to believe in him at all. God wanted to teach in an atmosphere of acceptance where the student would decide on his or her own.

He wasn't interested in using fear as a learning tool; indeed, his preferred style of teaching was based on a soft sell. Upon reflection, I think God adjusts the message to fit the audience.

God made it clear that there would be compassion, for-giveness, and justice as a consequence of how we'd lived our lives. He emphasized responsibility as something that was perfectly correlated with an ability to help others. Satisfaction in exercising compassion was a welcome by-product, but not a necessary condition, for doing whatever work was called for. The magnitude of the contribution was secondary. The actions of our lives will determine how valu-able our presence has been. Responsibility rests solely with anyone who is capable of helping someone else in need.

If we view an aspect of bravery as a willingness to reveal one's true self to others, then God is indeed coura-geous. He wants to be understood as a vulnerable being that has his own limitations. God is burdened, tired, and even depressed at times. He dared say that his own sur-vival depended on our help. He repeated a few times that being a good person was a matter of both common sense and knowledge.

God reminds us that he's here for the long run while our lives will end quickly enough. There was more to the story. The spiritual resources that God represents are in danger of being strained both by population demands and political/religious forces that have the potential to cause harm in the greatest magnitude.

Timing is everything in my work, and I suspect it is in

God's as well. Could it be as simple as that God sees what's up ahead and he's putting people together in certain ways in hopes of changing direction?

God's clever. I think he wants the reader to consider these points and act on some of them or not according to one's own will. I think God's unconcerned as to whether you believe any or all of it. He is *very much interested* in you thinking for yourself.

At first glance, that might seem naïve, simplistic, and reductionistic. In a skeptical world, it could even be considered suspect.

Yet, upon closer examination, there's genius imbedded in simplicity, and we know it. God teaches us that the most complex human systems are easily managed through tolerance, cooperation, and compassion. I believe God once said in one of our sessions that it wasn't rocket science.

In the end, I came to realize one main truth as God's shrink. It underscored everything God was saying between the lines.

God, the master choreographer and producer, needs us to help him realize his dreams and help keep *his* hope alive.

It's the least we can do.

Book Discussion Questions

1. *Do you think definitive proof of God's existence or nonexistence will ever be discovered?*

2. *In spite of their differences, why do so many religions share a number of common denominators?*

3. Richard is ambivalent about his religious roots: "I'd grown up in a Catholic family and been confused for some time about religious matters. I'd even occasionally attended the Unitarian Fellowship, a spiritual refuge camp of sorts, but eventually returned to my Catholic roots. I enjoyed the traditions, though I felt strangely detached from them. I'd look around church every Sunday and think that everyone else understood except for me." *What religion were you raised with and did you, in any way, feel*

detached? What religious rites felt foreign to you? What religion are you now, and how does your religion help you understand your life better?

4. *In session two, Gabe and Richard discuss the image of God as a perfect being. In your opinion, does God have to be perfect?*

5. As is revealed in session six: "My power is enhanced by good, positive energy, and it's depleted through evil, negative energy. There is no such thing as too small a contribution. Conversely, there's no negative action, no matter how seemingly insignificant, that doesn't weaken us." *Could God's actual well-being depend on human action or inaction?*

6. In session three, Gabe tells Richard: "There's some great choreography going on, so yes, lots of things fit into a bigger scheme. There are random events, too." *In your own life, do you have an example of some "great choreography"—a time when you couldn't explain something away as coincidence? What happened?*

7. *Do we have a psychological need to believe in God and an afterlife to make sense out of life?*

8. *Does everyone have some degree of free will?*

9. As Gabe explains in session six: "Good and evil are self-evident. It may require some work to get past some of the smoke and mirrors, but the clarity of what is right and wrong is there if you look closely enough. They're forces of energy that reside both within people and between them. It's an empirical truth that's based on a simple observation of life. *Is the concept of what it means to be a "good person" universal?*

10. *Are "good" and "evil" real forces at work in the world or just human constructs?*

11. *If heaven exists, would an atheist be able to get in if he or she had been a good person?*

12. *If you had an opportunity to speak with God, what three questions would you want to ask?*